Generation R:
A Retirement Nation at Risk

Generation R:
A Retirement Nation at Risk

How You Can Escape the Coming Retirement Crisis

Jeffrey W. Helms, CFA

Author of *What Great Investors Know*

iUniverse, Inc.

New York Bloomington Shanghai

Generation R: A Retirement Nation at Risk
How You Can Escape the Coming Retirement Crisis

iUniverse books may be ordered through booksellers or by contacting:

iUniverse
1663 Liberty Drive
Bloomington, IN 47403
www.iuniverse.com
1-800-Authors (1-800-288-4677)

Because of the dynamic nature of the Internet, any Web addresses or links contained in this book may have changed since publication and may no longer be valid.

The information, ideas, and suggestions in this book are not intended to render professional advice. Before following any suggestions contained in this book, you should consult your personal accountant or other financial advisor. Neither the author nor the publisher shall be liable or responsible for any loss or damage allegedly arising as a consequence of your use or application of any information or suggestions in this book.

ISBN: 978-0-595-45914-8 (pbk)
ISBN: 978-0-595-90214-9 (ebk)

Printed in the United States of America

The cessation of work is not accompanied by cessation of expenses.

—Cato the Elder

Contents

Acknowledgements

Indira Ghandi once said there are two types of people in the world—those who do the work and those who take the credit. It was her advice that you should try to be in the first group, as there was much less competition.

There are a number of people who deserve the credit for helping me deliver this important message to you.

First, I'd like to thank my peers. To all the competent qualified advisors out there who wake up every day with one goal—to help their clients succeed— you have my gratitude and respect. Keep fighting the good fight. Thanks also to the dedicated staff of our firm, because they know that they are making a vital difference in the lives of our clients.

I'd also like to thank a host of financial professionals like Nick Murray, Warren Buffett, Bill Sharpe, and others who have shaped my thinking over the years. Many of the concepts and ideas in this book originate from their teachings. I'm simply trying to translate those pearls of wisdom into terms everyone can understand and use in their everyday lives.

To my father, who passed away one year into his retirement after a lifetime of serving the public, you have been my inspiration to try and help people plan well. We miss you, Dad. To Mom, who has served as my proofreader and sounding board for making difficult stuff easy to understand, thanks loads. And finally, thanks to my dear wife Candy for her unbending support and patience with my inability to multi-task, and to my daughter Lily for reminding me why planning for the future is important.

Introduction

As I write this, hundreds of people in this nation are waking up and exclaiming, "I'm retiring today!" Tomorrow, hundreds more will do the same. And so on. These exclamations will have a profound effect on individual's lives and on our country as a whole, and it is my belief that most of these people aren't prepared for what awaits them. When it comes to retirement, we are about to experience a confluence of events of historic proportions.

Somewhere along the way, we became a nation of perceived entitlement. We developed a belief that our employers, the government, and society owed us a comfortable living in retirement. Perhaps this belief evolved from our parents' and grandparents' experience, when things were less complicated. Times have changed.

If you are of the mind that a long, comfortable, worry-free retirement is a birthright, you should return this book immediately and get your money back. And best of luck to you. This book is about taking personal responsibility for your future. The government is not responsible for your personal happiness and financial security in retirement. Neither is your employer. Nor your relatives. It's all on you. After reading this book, the choices you make and the actions you take—or don't take—will be magnified over the rest of your life and the lives of your family. If that sounds harsh to you, good. It means you're paying attention.

Nadine Gordimer, the Nobel laureate, once said, "A good scare is worth more to a man than good advice." I didn't set out to pen a book which would cause sleepless nights, but as I researched this retirement revolution further, it became apparent to me that perhaps the only way to save an entire generation from themselves was to present the facts as they are and hope those facts will positively influence readers to think hard about their futures. I believe most people are rational. I also believe that, presented with irrefutable facts, most people have the ability to change their behavior in their own personal self interest.

I am reminded of an old parable. A traveler is walking through the countryside when he comes upon an old country store. A farmer sits by the pot-bellied stove smoking his pipe. At his feet lies an old hound dog, moaning and groaning. The traveler asks, "Why is that dog moaning?" The farmer glances down at the dog and says, "Cause he's layin' on a nail." The traveler asks, "Why doesn't he just get up and move?" The farmer considers the question for a moment, removes the pipe from his mouth, and says, "I guess it don't hurt bad enough."

If after reading the first section of this book you find out the nail hurts badly enough, you will find all the information you need to take personal responsibility for getting up and moving somewhere more comfortable. The end game for us all, of course, is a long, healthy, rewarding, enriching, and fulfilling life. The strategies, solutions, and tools in this book can help you get there if you choose to use them. Assuming you do take action and improve your circumstances using the strategies herein, there are only two possible outcomes. First, let's assume my research proves correct and things do indeed become difficult for many Americans in the future. You'll have prepared well by immunizing yourself against those challenges and can live out your days in comfort. If I am wrong and none of my predictions come to pass, you'll have more money and can curse me from the deck of your luxurious beach house as you enjoy the sun setting over the horizon. Either way, you win.

Section I

What gets us into trouble is not what we don't know.
It's what we know for sure ain't so.

—Mark Twain

1

Setting the Stage

I want you to imagine that you work at a lunch counter. This is a special lunch counter, in that everyone who shows up must be served a lunch. You cannot refuse service to anyone. On a typical day at lunchtime, there are a few dozen people milling about outside waiting for you to open the doors. Suppose you show up for work one day, and there are 12,000 people in line waiting for their lunch. You scramble to feed them all. The next day, those same 12,000 people arrive, but another 12,000 arrive with them. The third day, all 24,000 show up again, and another 12,000 are behind them. Imagine this pattern continues *every day for 18 straight years.* Welcome to the retirement revolution.

In the eighteen years between 1946 and 1964, roughly 79 million Americans were born. This is what we refer to as the Baby Boom generation, or, as I like to refer to them, Generation R. That means, on average, about 12,000 people were born each day for those eighteen consecutive years. How will you feed them all?

A few years ago, Sebastian Junger wrote a book titled, "The Perfect Storm". In it, he provided a detailed explanation of how a series of independent meteorological events came together to create the storm of the century—a storm so fierce, its power and devastation were beyond anything experienced before it. Each of these weather events, on its own, didn't pose a particular threat. But, when these elements combined, the resulting storm was virtually unsurvivable by anyone in its path.

In order to frame an understanding of what awaits you in retirement, you need to understand a series of factual events that are occurring. Taken alone, these independent events may be mildly worrisome, and I doubt you're losing any sleep over them. But, it's the way these events will *interact* with each other that will dramatically impact the future, much like Junger's perfect storm. Some of these facts aren't pretty, but stay with me, because facts generally yield conclusions. The conclusions you draw from this combination of factual events could very well determine how well you fare when it comes to your retirement years.

The events we'll explore that will affect each and every retiree are:

+ The Boomers Big Bang
+ The Longevity Revolution
+ The Healthcare Conundrum
+ Social (In)Security
+ The Pension Ice Age
+ The Saving and Investment Vacuum
+ The Financially Illiterate Masses
+ The Rear View Mirror Approach to Retirement

Remember, it's the convergence of these events that will shape our future in retirement, so pay close attention as we explore each one.

The Boomers Big Bang

The Baby Boom generation has had a profound and challenging impact on virtually every facet of our society. Their arrival led to a migration from cities to the suburbs in the postwar years and prompted a building boom in housing and schools. From 1934 to 1947, prepared baby food sales jumped from 400,000 cases to 15 million. As Boomers reached young adulthood, their tastes in music,

4

fashion, and politics altered the fabric of our national culture. In the 1950s, more than 100 million Hula Hoops were sold. College enrollment tripled between 1965 and 1975. As they entered the workforce, boomers created enormous demand for new products including the Ford Mustang and (sadly for many dads) the minivan. The shopping mall was born. The economic ripple effect led to the largest and most sustained economic boom in our history. As Boomers approach retirement, much is being written about the growth of active adult communities, the swelling volunteer ranks in society, and the mass-migration to Arizona, Florida, and other retiree-friendly areas of the country. More than 1,000 people per day move to the state of Florida. In my county alone, more than 80,000 homes are scheduled to be built in the next few years. So, what are the implications? The Boomers big bang refers to the way this mass of humanity will change their consumption and investment habits as they retire. Where they live, what they buy (and don't buy), how they travel, and how they vote will continue to change our national fabric. Just as the end of the industrial revolution resulted in migration from cities to the suburbs and left urban areas blighted, the migration of Boomers as they retire will create similar opportunities and challenges. But, a more ominous effect will be felt from the support systems upon which they plan to depend. History is a great teacher if we are willing to listen. We have had sixty years to anticipate the ripple effect of this wave of humanity on our government, on social services and on society in general as this generation reaches retirement, yet little has been done to prepare for it or abate the effects, as you will soon see.

The Longevity Revolution

If you were alive in the year 1000, you could expect to live—on average—to about age 25. Disease, war, plague, famine, and pestilence were rampant, and you had very little defense against them. But, as we evolved, the advances in medicine, healthcare, and technology dramatically expanded your lifespan. By 1900, you were expected to make it to age 47. Today, average life expectancy is around 89 and it grows each year.[1]

Average Life Expectancy

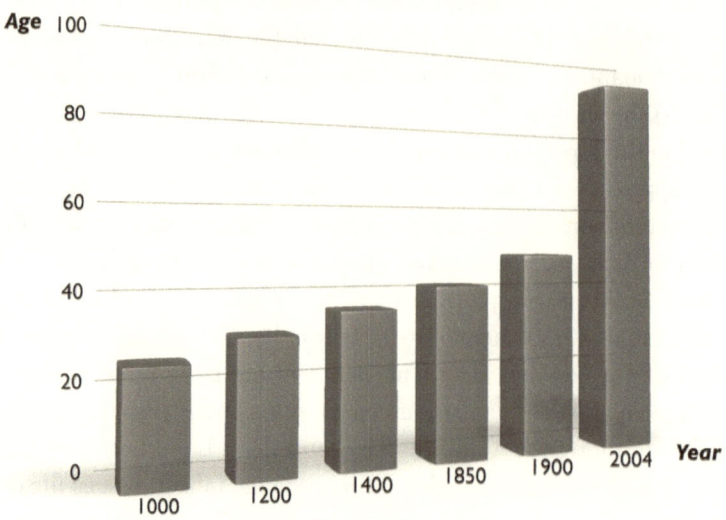

2000 Mortality and Expense Tables

What all this means, of course, is that Americans are living longer today than any time in history, and many of us will likely live well beyond our own anticipated life expectancy. We'll be active, healthy, and vital for much longer than we may think. I recently saw a bumper sticker on a golf cart that proclaimed, "70—The New 40" and I began to think about that. Because we're taking better care of ourselves, 70 is indeed much like what our parents probably felt like at age 40. We're living better, healthier, and longer.

A few years ago, a delightful woman named Jean Calment passed away. At 122, she was the oldest documented human being. Kelly Ferrin, a noted gerontologist, had the opportunity to interview her at age 117 to discern why she had recently given up smoking and drinking. Her reply? She felt that after 117 years, she had been living on the edge long enough. This is more than an amusing anecdote. It is a metaphor for how we will view a much longer life than the generations before us.

Today, there are more than 55,000 centenarians in the US. By 2050, "the number of US centenarians is expected to reach 834,000 and maybe even 1 million," according to Dr. Robert Butler, President of the International

Longevity Center in New York City. Hallmark, the maker of greeting cards, currently sells 85,000 100th birthday cards each year.

Now, hopefully a fact not lost on you is that the 79 million people in the Baby Boom generation will be living longer. Add to this the estimated 41 million retirees currently between the ages of 62–82, many of whom will also live longer. This will have a meaningful impact on us all as you will see later in the book. To quote Ken Dychtwald, the well-known author of the book, *Age Wave*, "The longevity revolution will have a greater impact on our lives than either the industrial revolution or the technology revolution of the last two centuries."

The Healthcare Conundrum

Medical science, better healthcare, and technology have cured a lot of things that kill us, thereby extending our lifespan, but they have not cured all the things that make us sick. Witness:

♦ A couple aged 65 today will need approximately $225,000 to fund their healthcare need in retirement.[2]

♦ In 2004, the increase in employer health insurance premiums was 11.2%.

♦ Between 2001 and 2003, national prescription medication spending rose 14%.[3]

♦ In 2003, Americans spent nearly $1.7 trillion on health care; by 2013, those costs are projected to double.[4]

♦ The Federal government estimated that, in 2004, there were 46 million Americans without health insurance.[5] This represents 15.7% of the population.

Perhaps the single greatest challenge we will face over the next three decades is maintaining the quality of health care provided to an aging population. Unlike prior generations, we can no longer turn to employers for retiree healthcare solutions, as this chart indicates.

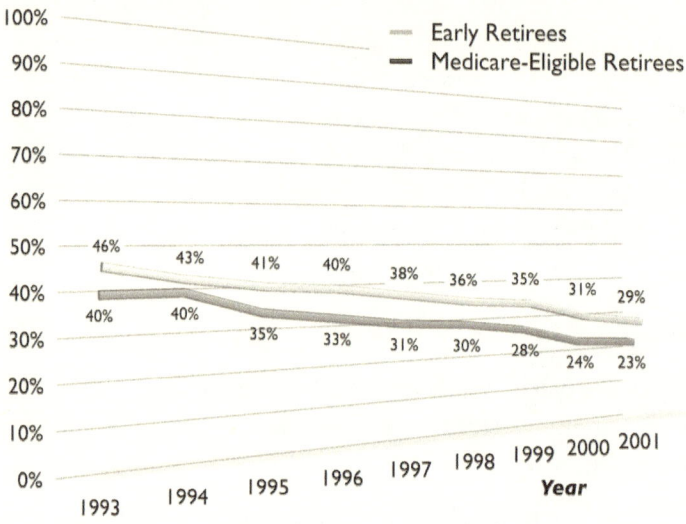

Employer-Sponsored Retiree Health Coverage Among Organizations with 500+ Employees

Source: Employee Benefit Research Institute Issue Brief 254

This challenge is not reserved for the private sector. State and local governments have recently begun to take aggressive steps to reduce the cost of providing healthcare benefits to retired teachers, police, firefighters, and other public workers. In December of 2006, the state of North Carolina reported $23.8 billion in unfunded liabilities for retiree healthcare, more than three times what the state owes in ordinary debt.[6] States are routinely either cutting benefits, extending current vesting requirements, or shifting the burden to Medicare for retiree healthcare expenses.

According to the governments audited financial statement released in December of 2006, Medicare's unfunded liability rose $2.6 trillion in 2006 to $32.3 trillion dollars. USA Today reported in May of 2006 that federal, state, and local governments owe at least $58.7 trillion—$510,677 per household—for Medicare, Social Security, civil servant health care, and other obligations.[7]

Unlike pension benefits, medical benefits are usually not protected by law and can be discontinued by state legislatures. All these events will force more retirees to depend exclusively on their own savings and Medicare to provide for their healthcare needs. It is difficult to imagine a solution that does not require citizens to take more personal financial responsibility for their own healthcare expenses in the coming decades.

Social (In)Security

In 1934, the nation was deep in the throes of the Depression. The traditional sources of economic security—assets, labor, family, and charity—had all failed to one degree or another. President Franklin Roosevelt would choose the social insurance approach as the "cornerstone" of his attempts to deal with the problem of economic security.

In 1935 he signed into law the Economic Security Act which created the Social Security Administration. The significance of this new social insurance program was that it sought to address the long-range problem of economic security for the aged through a contributory system in which the workers themselves contributed to their own future retirement benefit by making regular payments into a joint fund.

"We can never insure one hundred percent of the population against one hundred percent of the hazards and vicissitudes of life, but we have tried to frame a law which will give some measure of protection to the average citizen and to his family against the loss of a job and against poverty-ridden old age."

—President Roosevelt, upon signing the Social Security Act

While Social Security provided welcome assistance to a nation in need, the flaws of the program were first witnessed early on. Ida Mae Fuller was the first recipient of a monthly Social Security check. Mrs. Fuller paid a total of $27.00 into the system. Her first check was $22.54. Ida Mae lived to the ripe old age of 100 and collected more than $22,000 in benefits.[8] You don't need a PhD in Finance to discern this is an unsustainable gravy train.

How can our government's old age support system be so flawed? Well, it was developed upon the then accurate assumption that many more people were paying in than receiving benefits. At the inception of the Social Security Administration in 1935, the ratio of people paying into the system versus those taking out was 16:1. But things changed. In 1990, the ratio was 4.5:1. By 2030, it will be 2:1.[9] Unless reforms are undertaken, it is estimated that the Social Security system will be insolvent in 2042.[10]

9

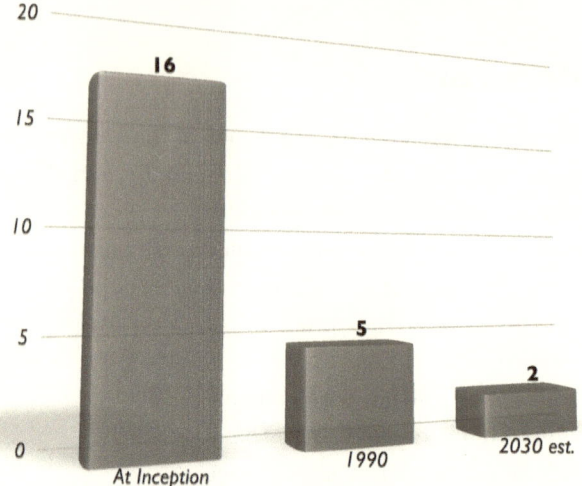

Number of People Paying into Social Security for Every Person Taking Money Out

1995 Annual Report of the Board of Trustees of the Federal Old Age and Survivors Insurance and Disability Insurance Trust Funds

It is important to note that the Social Security program was originally designed to provide *supplemental* income to a *minority* of Americans. Instead, it has become the *primary* source of income for the *majority* of Americans. It is estimated that more than 68% of Americans aged 65 and older rely on Social Security for 50% or more of their income and 39% rely on it for more than 90% of their income.[11] And the "lunch counter" hasn't really even opened yet for Generation R. This shift will have a profound impact on the system's ability to meet the needs of future retiring Americans.

It is somewhat interesting and ironic to note that the basis for our Social Security system was derived from Germany, which enacted the first old age pension under Chancellor Otto Von Bismarck in the late 1800s. As of November 2006, Germany's Cabinet had approved raising the official retirement age from 65 to 67 in order to cut state spending and pension costs.[12] You can be sure that politicians in the US will be closely watching this development overseas as a possible solution to some of our challenges. It is indeed difficult to imagine a remedy for our domestic program that does not contain the same elements.

The Pension Ice Age

For decades, a substantial number of Americans depended upon employer-funded pensions to provide a source of guaranteed income in their golden years. Coupled with Social Security, pensions provided assurance that regardless of how long you lived, you and your family could receive a monthly check as a reward for your years of contribution.

Beginning in the 1980s, however, many companies began to strain under the weight of retirees who were living longer and their growing pension liabilities. Something had to be done. In 1985, more than 110,000 employers offered a defined benefit (aka "pension") plan. By 2005, the number had shrunk to 30,000 employers as the following graph indicates.[13]

Employers Offering Defined Benefit Plans
(in thousands)

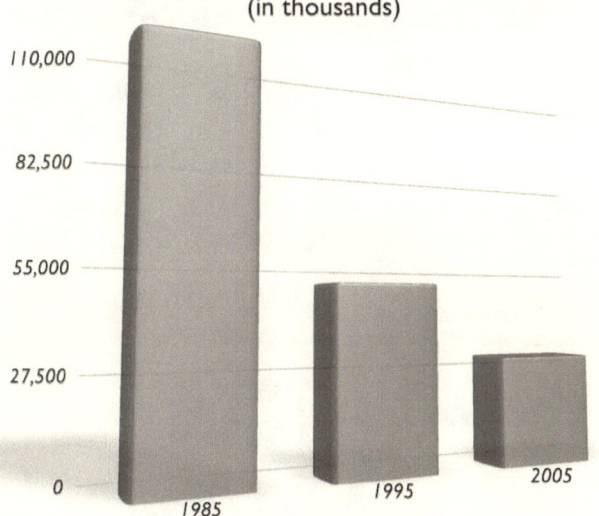

"The Incredible Shrinking Benefits," *Business Week*, July 25, 2005

Gradually, the burden for retirement planning has shifted to employees through the advent of defined contribution ("DC") plans. You know these plans by a series of confusing numerical and alphabetical codes such as 401(k)s, 403(b)s, 457 plans, etc. These plans differ from pension plans, in that their contributions are funded by the employee (and sometimes the employer) to determine potential future retirement benefits. It is worth noting here that this represents a transfer of risk from the employer to the employee. In pension plans, the employer or issuer of the pension benefits absorbs mistakes in funding requirements. In effect, they make good on it for the employees. In the future, the employee will absorb mistakes in their funding requirements. It is unsettling to note that even state and local pensions, long protected by either union contracts or constitutional guarantees, are being quietly challenged. Some have already reduced workers' pensions on the grounds that their pensions cannot sustain the weight.[14] According to Dereck Guyton with Mercer's Human Resources Consulting, the nation's cities and states have promised a total of about $1.4 trillion in commitments. Funding for these obligations is typically derived from your taxes. Take a look at the main reasons both public pension and private pension plans are being discontinued.

DB plan sponsors are closing or freezing their plans primarily because of the following:

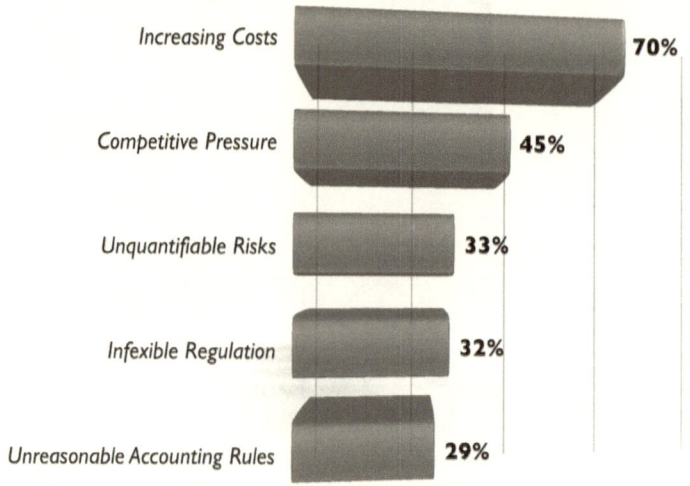

Increasing Costs	70%
Competitive Pressure	45%
Unquantifiable Risks	33%
Infexible Regulation	32%
Unreasonable Accounting Rules	29%

Source: Pensions & Investments, 2007

So, if employers have shifted the responsibility for funding retirement to employees, how are we doing at it? Unfortunately, this shift from involuntary retirement savings in pensions to voluntary savings in defined contribution plans has not been accompanied by the training and education necessary for most people to succeed, as you will see.

The Savings and Investment Vacuum

As if the foregoing facts aren't disturbing enough, the personal savings rate in the U.S. has steadily declined over the past few decades to about 2%. In fact, only two industrialized nations have lower savings rates than the United States. By contrast, Germany's personal savings rate is 11% and France's is 10.2%.[15]

According to the Credit Union National Association, credit union balances as a percentage of average household deposits have declined from 15.1% in 2001 to 2.5% in 2006. Mark Zandi, chief economist at Moodys.com, estimated the national savings rate in the first quarter of 2006 across all households was minus 1%.[16]

Personal Savings as a Percentage of Disposable Personal Income, 1950-2004

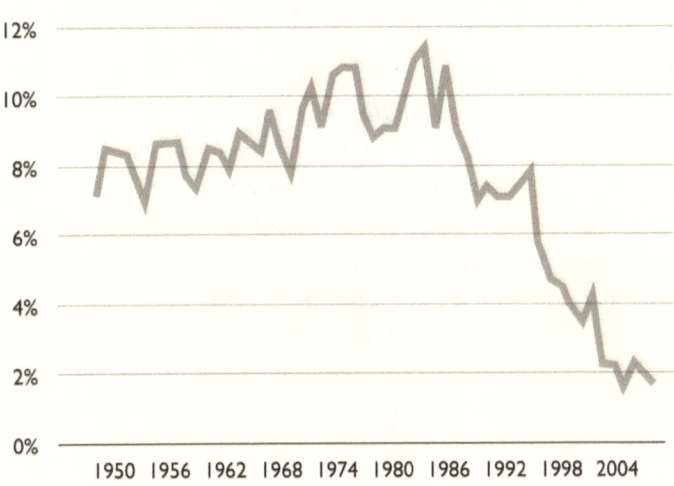

National Income and Product Accounts (NIPA's), U.S. Bureau of Economic Analysis, Sept. 2005

When we look at retirement savings alone, the news gets worse. Today, the median balance for all 401(k)s is approximately $35,000. Among those aged 55–64, the median balance is approximately $60,000.[17] Americans are simply not saving enough in personal retirement accounts to offset the changes occurring in government and employer funded programs. The 2004 Survey of Consumer Finances shows that 21% of eligible workers fail to participate in employer based defined contribution plans. Only 11% of workers participating contribute the legal maximum. Of those earning $40,000–$60,000, less than 1% contribute the maximum amount. This shift of responsibility to employees has been underway for a couple of decades now and it doesn't appear most Americans have risen to the challenge. The dismal savings habits of Americans, particularly those within a few years of retirement, are not likely to sustain a 30-year retirement.

The Financially Illiterate Masses

One might presume that the thrusting of responsibility onto individuals comes with an assumption that they have the skills to accept it. This doesn't appear to be the case by a long shot. The Retirement Research Center at the University of Michigan has done extensive work on the financial literacy of Americans, and the results aren't encouraging. Witness:

> *Gustman and Steinmeier (2004) show that only half of earlier respondents could identify what type of pension plan they had (defined benefit, defined contribution, or hybrid) and fewer than half could identify when they would be eligible for early or normal retirement benefits. Information about Social Security is also scanty. Only two-fifths of respondents could venture a guess about their expected Social Security benefits and many respondents knew little about program rules ... over half of current workers expect to become eligible for full Social Security benefits younger than they actually will (at age 65 or before). Thus, households are overall uninformed about the critical variables that should enter any saving plans.*[18]

In addition, a recent study by John Hancock Financial Services revealed the following insights:

- ♦ 38% of respondents said they had little or no financial knowledge.
- ♦ 40% of respondents incorrectly believed that a money market fund contained stocks.
- ♦ Two-thirds of respondents did not know that it is possible to lose money in government bonds (if you liquidate prior to maturity).

♦ Respondents on average believed that employer stock was less risky than a stock mutual fund.

How does this shocking lack of financial literacy translate in real life? A study prepared for the Nebraska Public Employees Retirement System (PERS) found that from 1983–1999 that system's pension plan (which is managed by pension trustees and professional money managers) generated an average of 11% annually, but the system's defined contribution plan participants (managing their own money) experienced returns of 6% over the same time period.[19] This is consistent with many current studies of average investor returns versus market returns in general. Giving people total responsibility for their financial future without the tools to succeed is akin to giving a fourteen-year old the keys to the Porsche. It's just not a good idea.

I suspect that readers with some level of financial acumen will dismiss these poor souls as lost causes. "Thank goodness I have the ability to manage my money," you may say. "Those poor folks will be left by the curb." Well, as you will see in the next chapter, this lack of financial literacy among your fellow citizens will likely end up costing you money in the long run, as government and social programs will be forced to pay the tab for such poor financial management and education. And they will pay for it with your tax dollars and the tax dollars of the generations that follow. No one is immune to the confluence of events I've described here. We will all be impacted in some way. Unless more Americans are prepared to educate themselves and seek professional assistance to help accumulate and manage their financial assets, this lack of literacy will create a tragic legacy for future generations.

The Rear View Mirror Approach to Retirement Planning

The last element I'll share with you isn't demographic. It's psychographic. And, it's the most important and potentially dangerous one in all this analysis. People, by nature, are extrapolators, which means that we think the future will be a logical extension of the past. We relate our past personal experiences to what we think the future will hold for us. (I will show you how this trait destroys your investment returns in a later chapter.) When it comes to retirement, our frame of reference is, of course, our parents and grandparents. In the 1970s, the average age of retirement was 65 and average life expectancy was around

8–10 years beyond that. Your parents and grandparents probably had very nice pensions, Social Security, and enough savings to live modestly, if not comfortably, for their life expectancy.

Today, the average age of first retirement is around 58.[20] If average life expectancy is, say, 89 and growing, that means on average you'll spend perhaps thirty years in retirement. So, in the last three decades, we have tripled to quadrupled the amount of time we will spend in retirement compared to our parents or grandparents. This is most certainly not your father's retirement. Yet, many seem to be planning as if it is. According to the 2005 National Survey of Employers and Employees, the average person plans for 19 years of post-retirement living. Only 37% of people surveyed are planning to live more than 21 years upon retirement.[21]

So, let's review what these facts reveal:

♦ 12,000 people are, on average, reaching retirement age every day.

♦ This group of people will, on average, live longer than anyone in human history before them.

♦ They will require quality healthcare during their retired lives, the cost of which increases each year.

♦ Government and social services for this group are already under significant strain, even before the bulk of them qualify for benefits.

♦ Corporate employers are shifting the burden for retirement savings onto the worker, and for many of them, it may be too late to comfortably accept the burden.

♦ The savings and personal investment accounts of most Boomers are woefully under funded if they exist at all and will likely not support a thirty-year retirement.

♦ People on average may not have the experience, capacity, or interest to successfully manage their own financial futures.

♦ People generally expect their future to look like their recollection of the past, and many underestimate how long they will live.

At best, this confluence of events is unsettling. Why is it we haven't considered these challenges as a group and addressed them before? Because these facts typically come to us one by one through the media. We read a headline one day about Medicare challenges, and the next day about a large company freezing their pension plan. No relation. It's not the media's job to connect the dots. As a result, we generally dismiss these events as noise. But, when one assembles these events into a cause and effect structure, the outcomes are worrisome at best, and more likely the perfect formula for a national crisis. Let me show you what I mean.

First, we learned that the largest segment of the U.S. population—79 million of them—are beginning to retire and will do so over the next 25 years, essentially crossing this threshold together. We also learned that they are living much longer than any generation before them.

Then, the facts teach us that this demographic shift is already stressing our government and social services programs and pension plans to their limits, and we've just gotten started. On January 1st, 2008, the first 12,000 baby boomers turned 62, qualifying for Social Security benefits. And 12,000 more will turn 62—*every single day*—for the next eighteen consecutive years. It also means that beginning in 2011, 12,000 people will qualify every day for Medicare benefits for eighteen straight years. And, they will consume a record amount of healthcare services.*

Regarding the government's ability to support both Social Security and Medicare benefits for future recipients, there is little disagreement on the plausible solutions. The Employee Benefit Research Institute, a highly regarded source of data on public policy and employee benefits, suggests:

> *"Since current tax revenues are projected to be insufficient to support these programs at their existing levels, some type of changes are likely to occur that could result in increased retirement age eligibilities, higher taxes, or in cutbacks of benefits." (October 2004)*

Perhaps the most watched man in politics and fiscal policy is our current Federal Reserve Chairman Ben Bernanke. Care to hear what he has to say on the matter?

> *"... as the population ages, the nation must choose among higher taxes, fewer government programs, cuts in Social Security and*

---

* You want job security? Apply to be a switchboard operator at the Social Security Administration.

Medicare, a higher deficit, or some combination of those options."
(October 5th, 2006)

Now, were this news not bad enough, we also learned that a diminishing number of people will be able to depend upon pensions to support themselves. And, few members of this generation have adequate personal savings and investments for retirement, which will increase their reliance on the already overburdened government and social service infrastructure. Lastly and most tragically, we learned that by nature, people tend to project their past experience into the future. Most appear to be blissfully unaware that all the elements of the perfect storm are converging in the next few years to disrupt their retirement life. Let all that sink in and marinate for a moment.

What are the consequences? How will all of us live for the next 30 or 40 years? What will our lives be like? Have I gotten your attention? Good. Read on.

Chapter Summary:

♦ The future will most certainly not be like the past.

♦ The intersection of all these statistically undeniable events will create substantial challenges for those who prefer to drive toward their retirement by looking in the rear view mirror.

♦ Accepting personal responsibility for a successful retirement is incumbent on each and every one of us.

2

A Tale of Three Retirements

The media bombards us daily with images of a mid-fifties retirement filled with cruises, vacation homes, and endless rounds of golf. It's a life of leisure. Retirement is one long non-stop party and you're all invited. The facts we just reviewed, however, paint a very different picture for many planning to retire in the next decade or two. What might life look like for this generation down the road? Let's look into the not so distant future. Imagine its 2029, the last Baby Boomer has just reached age 65, and we are a changed nation. While the following is not necessarily a prediction, one might certainly see how some of these outcomes could occur:

♦ Medicare, crushed under the weight of 79 million new qualifiers in only 18 years, has become a form of socialized healthcare and provides for only the most basic needs. The Prescription Drug Benefit Plan launched in 2006 failed most Americans, and they are forced to make difficult decisions between expensive healthcare, medication and lifestyle needs. On average, one third of after tax household income is spent on healthcare. Medicare supplement plans are expensive, difficult to understand, and leave many with significant gaps in coverage. Healthcare companies, struggling under the weight of increased regulation, government mandated

20

subsidies, and rising costs, have either merged, pared down their offerings, or exited the business altogether. The government wrestles to balance the need for basic healthcare for all Americans with politically unpopular tax increases to support it. Private comprehensive healthcare programs are financially out of reach for many Americans. A record number of citizens have no health insurance at all.

♦ To avoid certain insolvency, Social Security has undergone extensive "reform", the politically correct term for a wholesale reduction in benefits. The qualifying age for partial benefits has risen from age 62 to 66 for those born after 1959, and full benefits now begin between ages 72 and 76. (Politicians spin this not as a reduction in benefits, but preservation of your benefits paid out over a much longer life. Ahem.) Benefits are now fully taxed at ordinary income tax rates, meaning the Social Security taxes you paid into the system while working (which reduced your take home wages) are now taxed fully again upon receipt. Disability and survivor benefits have also undergone changes, none of which favor the beneficiaries.

♦ Pension plans are a thing of the past for the vast majority of corporate employers. The shift from defined benefit plans (where the employer bears the risk) to defined contribution plans (where the employee bears the risk) is complete. Many public sector employees still have a pension, but providers struggle to match tax revenues against the liabilities and have reduced the benefits accordingly or installed hybrid defined contribution plans as well to shift responsibility to employees. Those retirees still receiving full pension benefits from the 1990s and early 2000s are considered the most fortunate of all.

Based on this plausible scenario, I believe Baby Boomers will end up divided into three distinct groups experiencing three very different retirements. These groups are distinguished by both their economic circumstances and their lifestyle. Let's call them Dependent Retirees, Working Retirees, and Independent Retirees, for reasons that will become apparent.

Dependent Retirees are so named because they are almost fully dependent upon government, social services, and family members for sustaining themselves. Let's meet Will and Carolyn, typical Dependent Retirees:

Will, age 66, worked for a two private employers his entire career. Carolyn, age 64, was a homemaker. Will has a modest $12,000 pension from the first employer, and a small 401(k) with a $19,000 balance from the second. Will collects $17,000 in Social Security benefits annually. They also have a small savings account with $2,000. They owe $30,000 on their mortgage on the smaller home they purchased to save money. Both rely on Medicare, and they spend $700 per month on prescription drugs for cholesterol and blood pressure medication for Carolyn. They drive an older car. They don't take vacations. They visit with family when they can afford to drive cross-country to see them. Their children send them $500 per month to help make ends meet. Without Social Security and Medicare, they would be completely reliant upon their family, which bothers them. Will worries that inflation continues to eat into their meager savings and estimates it will be gone in five years. He stays glued to CSPAN, looking for signs of relief from Congress.

Will and Carolyn will have a lot of company. Based on my estimates, as many as 40 million folks could end up as Dependent Retirees. In fact, it's estimated that 25 million baby boomers have net assets of less than $1,000 and household incomes less than the national median of $46,326.[24]

The second group is **Working Retirees**. The oxymoron presented by the title isn't lost on most people. A large number of Americans who either retire before age 65 or find themselves forced to retire due to health, family, or employer-based reasons, will find themselves "in the breach", meaning they are not old enough to qualify for Medicare and must pay for healthcare needs for a period of years until they do qualify. For those retirees not eligible for Medicare benefits, the news is worse. They must foot their entire annual healthcare expense indefinitely. Finally, many retirees with Medicare benefits will seek employment to supplement their out-of-pocket healthcare costs not covered under Medicare. As a result, many will return to the workforce. Their primary motivation in the new job search? Health insurance benefits. They will scour the newspapers looking for employment opportunities. Newspaper classifieds will be divided into two categories—those jobs offering health insurance and those that do not—to make the search easier. Employers offering health insurance will have a ready pool of qualified experienced applicants.

Jackie is 60, and her husband Frank is 61. Frank took early retirement at age 58 due to his health and Jackie had planned to retire at age 60. But, because Jackie's employer offers health insurance, she will likely work until age 65, when she can qualify for Medicare. The cost of health insurance for both of them today would consume nearly half of their monthly income from Frank's pension and Social Security. They have modest savings and little debt and could live modestly without healthcare costs, but Frank is considering going back to work to save more money. They both believe they may end up working until age 70 to save more retirement dollars and offset healthcare costs.

I estimate another 20 million people could join the ranks of the permanently employed or Working Retirees.

The third group, **Independent Retirees**, have a more optimistic future. They saved substantially for retirement in their employer sponsored plans, IRAs, and personal savings accounts, and took personal responsibility for their futures.

Craig is 66, and Ellen is 65. Craig worked for two employers, has no pension, but managed to save $700,000 in his 401(k) plans over thirty years and another $200,000 in personal savings. He also has $75,000 in company stock in his IRA. He receives $17,000 in Social Security income. Ellen became a teacher after the kids were out of the house, and has $150,000 in a 403(b) plan and an $8,000 annual pension. They have no mortgage. They both rely upon Medicare for basic healthcare, but own private supplement plans to defray the cost of prescription medication and provide for all their needs. They purchased a small beach cottage in the early 2000s, where they spend their summers. They use Craig's Social Security income to pay for the cottage and to travel to Europe each year. They visit their children and grandchildren often. They purchase a new car every four years and use their savings to live the retirement life they imagined. In fact, their biggest financial concern is taxes, which continue to rise to pay for the social programs for dependent retirees.

Craig and Ellen have less company. Under the scenario described earlier, I would estimate less than 20 million people from Generation R would be categorized as Independent Retirees. You will note that Craig and Ellen are roughly the same age and receive the same social and government benefits as Will and Carolyn, but they do not depend upon them to support their lifestyle. They took personal responsibility for their future.

The latest research supports this view to a degree. The University of Michigan's Research Retirement Center's 2006 report, Baby Boomer Retirement Security: the Role of Planning, Financial Literacy, and Housing Wealth, showed that the distribution of net worth among early Baby Boomers is quite skewed; those in the top 25th percentile had over 10 times the net worth ($400,000) of households in the bottom 25th percentile ($37,000). This would indicate that unless something changes in our savings patterns soon, many people will find themselves working much longer than they anticipated or worse, dependent upon government and social services for the majority of their retirement income.

The purpose of the previous hypothetical exercise is to try and give you a glimpse of the future, and bring it back into the present while you can still do something about it. I realize that the scenario of becoming a Dependent or Working Retiree isn't very appealing, but there's a very real likelihood many people will end up there if they don't take personal responsibility for changing their future.

If all of this is too distressing to contemplate, you could take the more direct route to retirement planning like Timothy J. Bowers. On May 1, 2006, Mr. Bowers handed a teller a stickup note, got four $20 bills, and gave them over to a security guard at the bank, explaining that it was the guard's day to be a hero. At his trial,* he told the judge he was 63, unemployed, could not find work or affordable health insurance, and would appreciate a three-year sentence, so upon his parole at 66 he could thereby collect Social Security. He got it.

Mr. Bowers solved his income and healthcare gap in one fell swoop. He gets quality health coverage and three squares a day for the next three years. The prosecutor, Dan Cable, summed it up: "It's not the financial plan I would choose, he said, but it's a financial plan."

---

*   I am not making this up. See the article titled "Robber gets wish: 3 years in prison" published in the October 12, 2006 edition of the Columbus Dispatch.

Chapter Summary

♦ The next 25 years will see retirees falling into one of three lifestyle categories.

♦ In the first two groups, the quality of life will likely be less satisfying than they envisioned. The third group will experience higher satisfaction in their overall quality of life.

♦ Taking personal responsibility and making changes now could dramatically influence the group in which you end up.

Section II

There are risks and costs to a program of action.
But they are far less than the long-range risks and
costs of comfortable inaction.

—*John F. Kennedy*

3

The Five Key Risks
You'll Face in Retirement

If you are planning to retire soon or have retired in the recent past, you probably have many short-term questions on your mind. "Should I take up golf?" "Where would I like to travel?" "Should I fish today or tomorrow?" "Should we pretend we're not here when the kids call?" These are all perfectly normal in the short run. But, what about the long run? For the vast majority of people, the mother of all long-term questions is this:

"Will I be okay?"

To answer the question, you must identify the possible things that could make you "not okay". The things that could seriously disrupt your plans. This can be difficult, because it's not the snake you see that bites you; it's the one you don't see. Based on my experience and the research of a multitude of academic and financial institutions, there are five key risks we will all face in a long retirement. Before I describe them, let me offer you an analogy:

If you learned that you and your family faced a risk of serious disease from five new viruses, and medical researchers indicated there was a better than even chance you would be exposed to those viruses in the next few years, what would you do? If you're like most of us, you would head straight to your physician and get vaccinated against all five threats, correct? Well, your financial health in retirement is no different. If you can focus your efforts on immunizing yourself and your family against these five threats, you can spend your retirement years enjoying the fruits of your efforts.

One note of importance here: when it comes to planning for today's retirement, conventional investment wisdom is most certainly not your friend. You'll see what I mean. Here we go.

The trouble with being poor is that it takes up all of your time.

—*Willem de Kooning*

4

Risk #1: Outliving Your Assets*

Let me clarify something. It would be virtually impossible to truly outlive all your assets. If you receive a pension from your previous employer (and elect a life or life with survivor option for payment), you theoretically cannot outlive it assuming the company or government entity that owes you the pension remains solvent. If you receive Social Security benefits, you theoretically cannot outlive your benefit, assuming the Social Security Administration can continue to pay them. What we find more often is that the risk is not actually outliving every penny you have; it is the loss of dignity and independence that comes from making hard decisions about your lifestyle due to a lack of resources. We witnessed this in the examples of both Dependent and Working Retirees.

In the past, I have performed educational retirement workshops in my hometown for the Council on Aging, a non-profit agency that provides services to older adults. Some of these services include subsidized lunches, Meals on Wheels, and free groceries for those in need. Pat O'Connell, Director of Operations, tells me that as the month progresses, the number of people who utilize their services grows substantially. When I inquired why, I was told it is because many local retirees cannot make their Social Security or pension check last an entire month and need help to bridge the gap. I would submit

---

* The good news: you haven't expired! The bad news: your checkbook did.

to you that waiting at the mailbox every month for your Social Security check because the cupboard is empty is effectively the same as outliving your assets. That's no way to spend the rest of your life.

It's no wonder this is the first risk many pre-retirees face. Witness the following survey results:

♦   41% of Americans are worried they won't be able to maintain their standard of living in retirement.[22], yet only 42% of Americans have even tried to calculate how much income they will need in retirement.[23]

With priorities so misaligned, I suspect many retirees will face the prospect of outliving their resources. Of course, this would be a much easier calculation if you could determine precisely when you were going to expire. While no one can know for sure, we can turn to insurance companies, who make their profits by figuring out with frightening accuracy just when, on average, you are due to shake off your mortal coil.

In the following chart, you'll see the chances of living (on average) for another thirty years if you are 65 today. If you're younger than that, the numbers will be slightly higher depending upon your age.

From 65 Years Old

Age	75	85	95
Odds of Living	10 more years	20 more years	30 more years
Male (age 65)	84.5%	56.1%	21.9%
Female (age 65)	90.7%	69.1%	31.7%
One Member of a Couple (age 65)	98.5%	86.4%	46.7%

Source: 2000 Annuity Mortality Tables

So, we see that a male age 65 has, on average, about a one-in-five chance of living another 30 years. A female, aged 65, has about a one-in-three chance. What does this teach us? That husbands tend to die before their wives.*

The most important thing to remember is that insurance companies use averages to predict life expectancy. What this means is that, on average, half

---

*   A client of mine assures me it's because they want to, but I don't believe it.

the people will expire prior to these estimates. The other half will live beyond these estimates. If you are in the former group, you won't know it. If you are in the latter group, planning for it can mean the difference between a comfortable lifestyle and one filled with difficult decisions.

Let me tell you a story. Jackie and Mark came to see me about a year ago to explore some planning needs. Jackie is 84, and Mark is 85. They have a sizeable estate. After our visit, I recommended they see an elder law attorney, which they did. Jackie stopped by the office recently to visit. She was very emotional. "Mark has just been diagnosed with Alzheimer's," she said tearfully. "My biggest fear is that his dad also had it, and lived in an institution for fourteen years." As she left my office, she turned to me and said, "You know, we just never thought we would live this long." I can assure you, there are no sadder words to hear.

Chapter Summary

♦   Many of us will live longer than we think, and you would be wise to plan for a much longer life than you may expect.

♦   If you're wrong and you die earlier, you won't know it.

♦   If you're right, at least you'll be prepared.

In spite of the cost of living, it's still popular.

—*Laurence J. Peter*

5

Risk #2: Inflation*

If it was a disease, it would be called the silent killer. Inflation is insidious and creeps into every aspect of your lifestyle. Inflation is nothing more than a rise in the prices of goods and services. The effect of inflation, however, is a loss of your purchasing power. A dollar today will not buy a dollar's worth of goods tomorrow.

In 1950, the average cost of a house in the U.S. was $8,450. Gasoline was .17¢ per gallon. A year of tuition at Harvard was $600. A loaf of bread was .17¢.[24] Shall I continue?

When you retired at age 65 and died at 72, 3% inflation probably wasn't meaningful to you. But, as the following chart reflects, 25 years at 3% annual inflation means you will need more than twice your current income *just to maintain your current lifestyle*.

---

* This one is my personal favorite.

Inflation Over Time

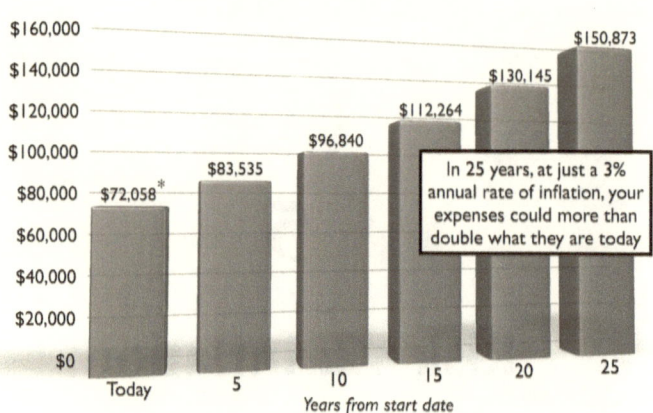

In 25 years, at just a 3% annual rate of inflation, your expenses could more than double what they are today

*$72,058 was the annual expenditure for individuals age 65+ with income greater than $70,000 from the U.S. Department of Labor, Bureau of Labor Statistics, Consumer Expenditures 2000 report.

Here is where conventional wisdom can hurt you. It was a common belief in the past that, as you got close to retirement age, you needed to move your assets into "safe" investments such as bonds and CDs. The notion here was that you couldn't afford to risk your hard earned money, and the yields from these secure investments would do just fine to supplement your income. This strategy may have been fine when your average life expectancy in retirement was five to ten years, but it is a dangerous notion if you plan to be around for a number of years, because inflation will erode your purchasing power. $10,000 today will not be worth $10,000 tomorrow. Here's an example:

> Let's say you have $200,000 invested in government bonds and CDs. Let's further assume that you withdraw 5% per year, or $10,000, to supplement your retirement income. You should be fine for the next thirty years, right? Well, you forgot about inflation and taxes. Historically speaking, this strategy has never sustained itself—after taxes and inflation—during any 30 year time period you wish to choose. You simply ran out of money.

Let's look specifically at CDs to understand this a bit better, since they seem to be the most popular retirement investment on the planet. The following chart reflects the gross return on CDs for the years 1980–2005, representing a 25-

36

year retirement. The far right column, however, reflects the real return on CDs *after taxes and inflation* for the same time period:[25]

Gross Versus Real Returns on CDs

YEAR	6 Month CD Rate*	Taxes**	Inflation***	Real Return
1980	12.95%	59.0%	12.52%	–7.21%
1981	15.76%	58.3%	8.92%	–2.35%
1982	12.55%	50.0%	3.83%	2.45%
1983	9.27%	48.0%	3.79%	1.03%
1984	10.67%	45.0%	3.95%	1.92%
1985	8.24%	45.0%	3.80%	0.73%
1986	6.51%	45.0%	1.10%	2.48%
1987	7.00%	38.5%	4.43%	–0.13%
1988	7.90%	33.0%	4.42%	0.87%
1989	9.08%	33.0%	4.65%	1.43%
1990	8.17%	33.0%	6.11%	–0.64%
1991	5.91%	31.0%	3.06%	1.02%
1992	3.76%	31.0%	2.90%	–0.31%
1993	3.28%	31.0%	2.75%	–0.49%
1994	4.95%	31.0%	2.67%	0.75%
1995	5.98%	31.0%	2.54%	1.59%
1996	5.46%	31.0%	3.32%	0.45%
1997	5.72%	31.0%	1.70%	2.25%
1998	5.44%	28.0%	1.61%	2.31%
1999	5.39%	28.0%	2.68%	1.20%
2000	6.63%	28.0%	3.39%	1.38%
2001	3.53%	27.5%	1.55%	1.01%
2002	1.78%	27.0%	2.38%	–1.08%
2003	1.19%	25.0%	1.89%	–1.00%
2004	1.80%	25.0%	3.25%	–1.90%
2005	3.80%	25.0%	3.84%	–0.99%

1. – *CDA Wiesenberger, 1/06.* ** *Highest marginal Federal income tax rate based on $100,000 of taxable income for a married couple filing jointly.* *** *Bureau of Labor Statistics, 2006.*

Now, forget the chart for a moment, and let's look in on a client conversation:

Client: *"I need a safe investment for my 25 year retirement."*

Broker: *"Great, I've got one for you right here. In the past twenty-five years, it's only had negative real returns to investors ten times, and in its best year it returned a princely 2.45% after taxes and inflation. How much would you like to buy?"*

Client: *"You need to see a mental health professional quickly. Where's the door?"*

And yet billions upon billions of retirement dollars flow into CDs annually. Don't get me wrong—CDs can be a perfectly suitable place to park some of your money for a shorter period of time, as you'll see later in the book. But, they are simply not designed to be a long-term retirement vehicle. Still don't believe me? How many 20-year CDs do you see in the local paper?

How does all this translate to your wallet? While a fixed rate of return for several years sounds like a stable investment, inflation erodes the buying power every year. Let's use an inflation rate of 3.1%, the historical average since 1925. Assume you put $100,000 into a 20-year government bond yielding 5%.

As you can see below, your $5,000 annual interest check from Uncle Sam will be worth $2,749 after twenty years. And, we haven't even calculated taxes into the equation.

The Buying Power of a Dollar Over Time

Inflation diminishes the buying power of a dollar every year. A 3.1% average inflation rate would reduce the buying power of $5,000 to just $2,749 in less than twenty years."

Hartford Life Insurance Company, 2005

For those readers who prefer a simpler explanation of the effect of inflation, try this little test:

1. Question: What will you do with all the money you have in retirement?

    Answer: Buy things.

2. Question: What have the prices of "things" done since the day you were born?

   Answer: Gone up.

Finally, the retiree in denial will proclaim, "Yes, yes, I know that inflation is a worry, but not for me! You see, I receive a Cost of Living Adjustment (aka COLA) on my pension and/or Social Security benefits periodically. Therefore, I am in fine shape."

Show me a cost of living adjustment to a pension or to Social Security that has kept pace with the rising cost of healthcare, energy, and food, and I'll refund every dime you paid for this book. Adjusted for inflation, of course.

Chapter Summary

♦ **Inflation is the silent assassin of your lifestyle in a long retirement.**

♦ **A dollar today will most certainly not be worth a dollar tomorrow, and fixed income sources run the risk of not keeping your purchasing power intact.**

I have enough money to last me the rest of my life,
unless I buy something.

—Jackie Mason

6

Risk #3: Low Returns and Poor Withdrawal Planning

Here's a history question:

Who was the first man to successfully summit Mount Everest?[*]

If you guessed Sir Edmund Hillary, you would be wrong. Many historians believe that George Mallory successfully climbed Mount Everest in 1924, almost 29 years before Hillary made his historic ascent. Why have most people never heard of him if he were truly the first man to climb up Everest? *Because he didn't make it down.* His body was found in 1999 below the Northeast Slope, frozen solid on his descent.

If you're smart, you've spent your entire life accumulating assets for retirement. But, as we'll see, the strategies you use to accumulate wealth don't work on the other side of life's mountain—the distribution phase. A stumble here can be disastrous.

---

[*] Think about it. I'll wait.

Low Returns

Once again, I note that the conventional wisdom that retirees should own only fixed income investments is fundamentally flawed if you plan to stick around for a while and wish to live comfortably. Often, I note that people preparing for retirement in a year or two have moved their assets into either money market type instruments or bonds. When I ask why, they explain that are getting ready to retire and are concerned about risk. Here's an important point to embrace:

Your investment time horizon is not your retirement date; it's the rest of your life.

Unless you plan to spend every penny the day you retire, why on earth would you do such a thing? Aren't you counting on those assets to grow and produce income for you for the rest of your life?

Let's look at average annual returns from 1926–2004 on stocks, bonds, and cash.[26] Note the gross returns versus net returns, *after taxes and inflation.*

**Returns Before and After Taxes and Inflation
1926 – 2004**

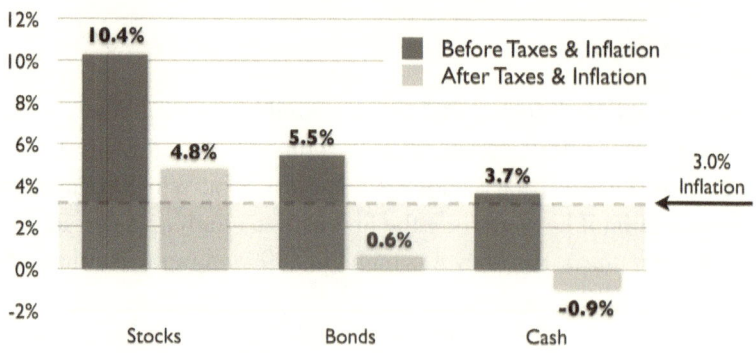

Assumes reinvestment of income and no transaction costs.
Hartford Life Insurance Company, 2005

And of course, this assumes no withdrawals. Imagine what happens when you withdraw 4% per year for income from your retirement assets sitting in money markets and bonds. As you can see, traditionally "safe" investments are anything but when it comes to protecting your purchasing power and producing a growing stream of retirement income. Remember, you're investing for the rest of your life, not the day you get your gold watch.

Poor withdrawal planning

For most of us, our investing efforts to date have been focused on accumulating assets. Now, the conversation is shifting. The newest frontier in retirement planning focuses on "distribution" or withdrawal planning. In short, how do we make sure that all we have accumulated lasts us as long as we need it to? Once again, we will see that conventional wisdom fails us here, as the strategies we have used for wealth accumulation do not work on the other side of the mountain. We have no way of knowing what future returns will be, but we know that those returns—good or bad—will have a dramatic impact on our ability to fund our retirement lifestyle. Specifically, *the sequence of our returns* will be a critical consideration. Let's assume for a moment we have two fairly astute investors—Bert and Ernie. Each has a well-diversified portfolio worth $250,000, which they have accumulated over their working lives. Each estimates they can earn an average rate of return on their portfolio of 7%. Both begin 5% withdrawals at retirement.

Here's where average rates of return can get you in trouble. The chart below reflects an average rate of return of 7% for both Bert and Ernie for a thirty year retirement:[27]

Sequence of Returns

Withdrawals agin at 62	Bert's $250,000 Portfolio Negative Returns Early		Ernie's $250,000 Portfolio Positive Returns Early	
	Hypothetical Annual Rate of Return	Portfolio A Year-End Value	Hypothetical Annual Rate of Return	Portfolio A Year-End Value
Age		$250,000.00		$250,000.00
62	-17.6%	$193,500.00	16.6%	$279,000.00
63	-12.8%	$155,857.00	7.4%	$286,771.00
64	-3.5%	$137,141.00	12.0%	$307,922.00
65	6.4%	$132,259.00	11.3%	$329,058.00
66	9.3%	$129,167.00	3.3%	$325,848.00
67	15.4%	$134,568.00	20.7%	$379,740.00
68	-3.0%	$115,605.00	3.3%	$376,313.00
69	7.1%	$108,440.00	8.8%	$394,055.00
70	16.9%	$110,932.00	9.7%	$416,444.00
71	6.7%	$102,054.00	14.3%	$459,686.00
72	7.2%	$92,608.00	9.7%	$407,478.00
73	11.9%	$86,320.00	7.2%	$505,272.00
74	12.1%	$78,943.00	14.9%	$562,735.00
75	8.1%	$66,981.00	9.1%	$595,588.00
76	12.0%	$56,111.00	-3.2%	$557,621.00
77	-3.2%	$34,841.00	12.0%	$605,061.00
78	9.1%	$17,953.00	8.1%	$634,013.00
79	14.9%	$0.00	12.1%	$690,067.00
80	7.2%	$0.00	11.9%	$750,905.00
81	9.7%	$0.00	7.2%	$783,051.00
82	14.3%	$0.00	6.7%	$912,939.00
83	9.7%	$0.00	16.9%	$927,073.00
84	8.8%	$0.00	7.1%	$968,943.00
85	3.3%	$0.00	-3.0%	$915,205.00
86	20.7%	$0.00	15.4%	$1,030,737.00
87	3.3%	$0.00	9.3%	$1,090,116.00
88	11.3%	$0.00	6.4%	$1,132,926.00
89	12.0%	$0.00	-3.5%	$1,065,507.00
90	7.4%	$0.00	-12.8%	$900,523.00
91	16.6%	$0.00	-17.6%	$712,574.00

Negative returns
early deplete savings
after 17 years

Positive returns early can extend
savings more thirty years despite
the same average rate of return

Prudential/American Skandia, 2006.

As you can see, experiencing poor returns early in retirement can have a dramatic effect on how long your nest egg may last with a set withdrawal rate. Bert, who had negative returns early in retirement, simply runs out of money at age 81. Ernie, who experienced positive returns early in retirement, has a much better result.

Note well: both investors had the same average annual return over retirement, but a big difference in outcomes due to the timing of those returns.

That's why withdrawal planning is so important in retirement planning; you simply can't "set it and forget it."

Chapter Summary

♦ Conventional wisdom dictated that retirees should largely own fixed investments, which have lower historical returns. But, if you plan to be around a while, you cannot ignore the effects of inflation and taxes on your overall returns.

♦ In addition, the prospect of unpredictable returns each year can have a meaningful impact on your outcome.

The avoidance of taxes is the only intellectual pursuit that carries any reward.

—John Maynard Keynes

7

Risk #4: The Tax Man Cometh ... Again and Again

Another bit of conventional wisdom is that your taxes will be lower when you retire. This was likely true for your grandparents and possibly your parents, but I would suggest the first few pages of this book should lead you to a different conclusion for the next generation. The good news? The government has decided to adjust the tax rates to more heavily tax the rich.

The bad news? You're rich. The Congressional Budget Office tracks who pays what and provides a wonderfully depressing series of tax charts for our review. My, what a difference a few decades makes:

Share of Total Federal Income Tax Liabilities by Income Level

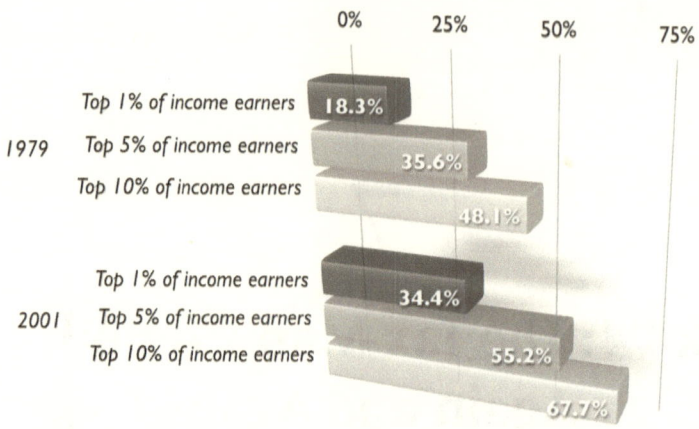

Congressional Budget Office, 2001

Now let's look at tax rates by household income.

Effective Federal Tax Rates by Household Income Category, 1997 to 2000

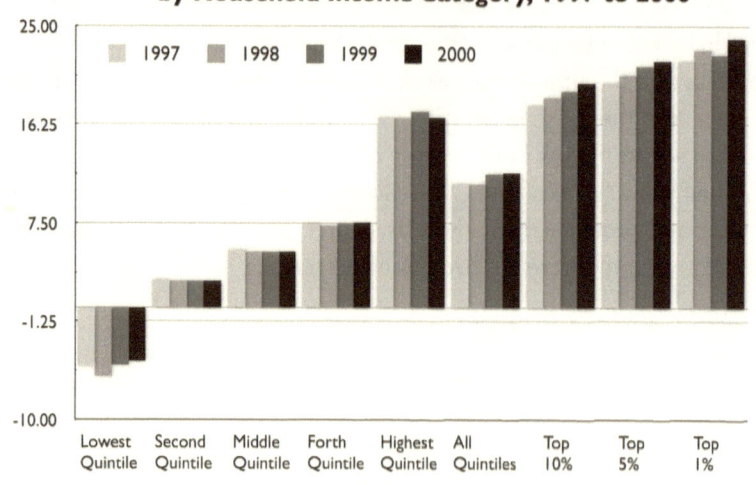

Congressional Budget Office, 2001

Lastly, take a look at this chart, which reflects effective federal tax rates by revenue source from 1997 to 2000.[28]

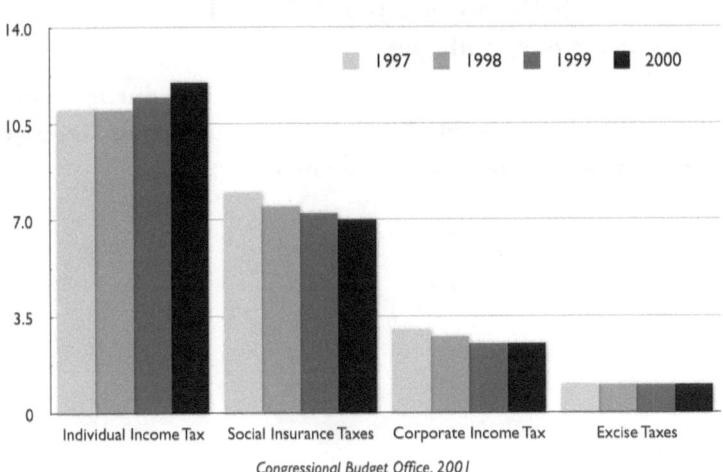

Effective Federal Tax Rates by Revenue Source, 1997 to 2000

Congressional Budget Office, 2001

Notice a pattern here? Taxes will be particularly meaningful in retirement for those who have uncontrollable sources of income such as pensions, Social Security, and mandatory IRA distributions. The risk, simply stated, is that your net retirement income after taxes may be less than you expect. Tax planning both prior to and in retirement will be an essential element for all of us. Here is a particularly articulate bit of tax strategy provided to us by the honorable jurist Judge Learned Hand:

> *"Anyone may arrange his affairs so that his taxes shall be as low as possible; he is not bound to choose that pattern which best pays the treasury. Nobody owes any public duty to pay more than the law demands."*

Managing when and how much tax you pay in your retired years by using every legal means at your disposal will have meaningful consequences on your lifestyle and your potential legacy to your heirs.

Chapter Summary

♦ Based on the undeniable economic challenges facing us, you would do well to plan for higher and not lower taxes during retirement. (If I'm wrong, you'll simply have more money. I'll assume that's okay with you.)

♦ Disregarding the effect of taxes prior to and during retirement can result in substantially less net retirement income and compromise your legacy to your heirs.

Be careful about reading health books.
You may die of a misprint.

—Mark Twain

8

Risk #5: Healthcare Costs

As I noted earlier, our medical advances have truly been amazing over the past century. Many of the illnesses that would kill us before our time have either been eradicated or are at least under control. But, many of the maladies that come with aging are still being researched, and the best we can hope for is to manage them and still maintain a decent quality of life. As the humorist P.J. O'Rourke noted, "The doctor says if I stop smoking and drinking, it will add ten years to my life. The problem is it adds them to the wrong end."

The Center for Retirement Research has conducted extensive studies on the financial challenges that healthcare presents to an aging nation. In a recent survey, 39% of terminally ill patients reported that healthcare costs caused moderate or severe financial problems. About half of Americans filing for bankruptcy in 2001 cited medical causes.

Comprehensive healthcare coverage will present perhaps the single largest risk we face in retirement. Many prefer to ignore this risk hoping for either divine or government intervention. The thought of depleting our savings and investments and, worse yet, becoming a burden to our families, is too uncomfortable to think about for long. Yet we ignore the problem at our own peril.

The spiraling cost of healthcare related expenses shows no signs of abating. Unfortunately, the cost-of-living increases built into Social Security, pensions, and other retirement benefits are generally based on the Consumer Price Index, a broad indicator of inflation. But, the rapid rise in healthcare expenses is greatly outdistancing those increases. Witness:[29]

Healthcare Cost Increase

Expense	Time Period	Cost Increase	Cost: 2002	Cost: 2025
Drugs	1/80 - 1/01	237%	$30 per prescription	$114 per prescription
Nursing Home	12/96 - 1/01	20%	$75,000 annually	$173,498 annually
Health care	1/80 - 1/01	274%	$520 monthly	$2,205 monthly

Estimated Health Care Payments as a Percentage of After-Tax Income

2000	2010	2020	2030
16%	24%	29%	35%

Bureau of Labor Statistics, Department of Commerce, 2002

The conclusion:

You will have to bear more of the expense of maintaining your health in the future.

According to the 2002 Health and Welfare report prepared by Fidelity Workplace Services, a couple who retired in 2002 at age 65 could need current savings of $160,000 to supplement Medicare and cover their out-of-pocket health care expenses in retirement. A couple retiring at age 60 would need to plan on about $210,000 over the course of their retirement. These estimates don't include possible long-term care needs.*

Contrary to popular belief, long-term care is not covered by Medicare or typical employer-based retiree healthcare plans. Costs for one year of care can range from $33,000 in Louisiana to over $91,000 in Connecticut.

---

* Long-term Care goes by a number of names such as nursing home care and others.

Roughly 60% of Americans now turning 65 will be admitted to a nursing home at some point in their lives. Half of them will stay six months or less, but about 1 in 10 will stay three years or more.[30]

In 2004, the average daily rate in a long term care facility for a semi-private room was $169, or about $61,000 per year. Today, the average rate for a private room is $206 per day, or $75,190 annually.[31]

Unless you have made arrangements to cover these costs through some other means they will be borne by you or your family.

Chapter Summary

♦ **It is reasonable to assume that much of the financial responsibility for quality healthcare in retirement will shift to individuals. And, costs will likely continue to rise. Planning for this now may help ease the burden in the future.**

*If you haven't the strength to impose your own terms upon life,
you must accept the terms it offers you.*

—T.S. Eliot

9

Taking Responsibility

We don't know how long we'll live; what future inflation rates will be; what our investment returns will be; how much we'll need for healthcare; or how future tax rates will affect our net retirement income. But, these risks have spawned a cottage industry focused on the economics of retirement. There is much research being performed to help retirees deal with these challenges. What we do know is that ignoring these five risks will lead countless Americans down the path to a dependent or permanently employed status in retirement, a significantly reduced quality of life, or perhaps both.

The responsibility for ensuring you and your family are effectively immune from these five risks rests with you. Period. End of sentence.

The government is not responsible for your financial welfare, nor your employers; nor your parents, or your children.

If it is not yet evident that you need to take control and responsibility for your retirement success, then perhaps you are the dog laying on a nail in the country store, moaning. Do you really want to wait until it hurts bad enough to get up and move?

In order to prepare yourself and take responsibility for your destiny in retirement, you need to understand the building blocks of good decision-making for investing. You need to be financially literate. In the next few chapters, you can get the knowledge you need. If you have no investment experience, relax. This information relies more on common sense than complicated charts and graphs or a degree in finance. Should you already have a decent understanding of investing basics, I'll wager you have a few horror stories that will fit nicely into what you are about to learn, so these chapters will benefit you as well.

Once you gain some financial literacy, we'll move on to strategy. Then, you'll be on your way to a rewarding and a fulfilling retirement.

Section Summary

- **The 5 key risks you'll face in retirement:**

  Risk #1: Outliving Your Assets

  Risk #2: Inflation

  Risk #3: Low Returns and

  Poor Withdrawal Planning

  Risk #4: The Tax Man Cometh ...

  Again and Again

  Risk #5: Healthcare Costs

- **Who is responsible for protecting your retirement? *You* are!**

Section III

An investment in knowledge always pays the best interest.

—*Benjamin Franklin*

10

Transforming Yourself into a Great Investor

In my first book, *What Great Investors Know*, I distilled out the basic knowledge you need to be successful in investing for retirement. "No thank you, Jeff," you say. "I have no desire to study numbers and deal with complex calculations." Well, as you'll learn, it's less about deciphering complex calculations and more about using your head. These simple, common sense lessons you are about to learn have been tested by time, and they work. They are rooted in both rigorous academic study and in practice. There are no formulas to learn, no secret incantations to recite, and no magic software programs to buy. This is basic stuff, folks, and it works splendidly.

Before we begin exploring the lessons of Great Investors, let's get one thing straight:

Regardless of your age, wealth, or investment experience, there are only three goals of investing.

That's right: *only three*. And, they apply to every single person on the planet. I will now impart to you what is quite possibly the most important element to becoming a Great Investor (so pay attention).

The Three Undeniable Goals of all Great Investors:

1. Comfortable worry-free income as long as we live.

Most people would agree that ensuring that their standard of living is maintained or enhanced in their retirement years is a primary goal. They also wish to ensure that their pre-retirement years are ones where their living standard continues to grow, and post-retirement—whether starting at 55 years of age or 70 years of age—is comfortable and worry free from a financial perspective. Who doesn't dream of a lifestyle of spontaneous trips to Europe, a new car or boat, or a cottage at the beach? Regardless of our age, we're all investing for the same reason—income at some future point for our families. Accumulating wealth isn't perpetual, it's ultimately to produce income for someone, and that's the single goal we all share.

2. Having ample financial resources to better the lives of children, grandchildren, family members, or others who are important to us.

This goal provides us with a great sense of self-worth, as we are helping those most important to us: ensuring that our children and grandchildren can attend the college of their choice; assisting our children in the purchase of their first home; helping a family member during a time of crisis; ensuring there are ample resources to assist aged or ailing parents, siblings or other family members; and intervening in the lives of those we love is a most basic and fundamental goal aside from our own personal needs.

3. Creating a legacy for family members, charities, or institutions of our choice.

Building wealth for the purpose of passing along a living legacy to family members is an important value, as is ensuring that the church, charity, or other institution of our choice is recognized. Many people achieve a sense of great self-worth as a result of creating a lasting legacy. Knowing that our names and deeds live on long after we're gone gives us great satisfaction and peace of mind.

That's it. This is the stuff of life. All other "goals" you may describe are not end goals themselves, but simply a means to an end, and will fit comfortably underneath one of these.

Don't believe me? Let's walk through a couple of examples.

Beth and Her Advisor

Advisor: *What is important to you about your planning needs?*

Beth: *I want to acquire lots of wealth.*

Advisor: *Okay, why is that important?*

Beth: *I don't want to have to depend on anyone else.*

Advisor: *Why is it important for you not to have to depend on anyone else?*

Beth: *Because I've always been independent.*

Advisor: *Got it. What does that independence do for you?*

Beth: *It gives me choices.*

Advisor: *Like what, for instance?*

Beth: *I can do what I want to do, when I want to do it, for the rest of my life, and not worry about having enough income to do it.*

Advisor: *So, it gives you the financial freedom to live a worry free lifestyle for the rest of your life, right?*

Beth: *Right, that's it.*

So, you see, Beth's goal isn't really "wealth accumulation," it's a worry-free lifestyle with plenty of income for the rest of her life.

Accumulating wealth is a means to a goal, not the goal itself.

Fred and His Advisor:

Advisor: *What are your objectives?*

Fred: *I'm paying too much in taxes and I want to find out how to pay less.*

Advisor: *Okay, why is it important to you to pay less in taxes?*

Fred: *Because I hate giving Uncle Sam so much of my hard earned money.*

Advisor: *I see. So, if you gave Uncle Sam less money, you'd have more for yourself—right?*

Fred: *You got it.*

Advisor: *Let's assume you paid less in taxes. What would you do with all that extra money?*

Fred: *Well, I'd invest it.*

Advisor: *Okay. For what?*

Fred: *Well, we don't really need it for retirement, because we're pretty well set. But, I want to make sure the kids and grandkids are taken care of too.*

Advisor: *I see. So, keeping more of your tax dollars to help take care of your family is your goal?*

Fred: *Yeah, that's right.*

Again, we see that Fred's goal isn't really to pay less in taxes. It's to provide a legacy for his family, either now or after he's gone, to better their lives. Paying less tax isn't the end—it's a means to a greater end.

That's it. Pretty simple, really. Whether you're a self-made millionaire, or simply trying to start saving, we all share the same three basic goals. Thinking about these goals in advance can greatly simplify your planning and clarify much of the confusion associated with investing.

Now might be a good time to pull out the yellow pad and list out what's really important to you as you think about the *Three Undeniable Goals of Great Investors*. If you will start with what's really important in life, you find you gain a lot of clarity. Once you can commit to your true goals, getting there becomes a lot easier.

There are essentially five elements to becoming a Great Investor, and they have been proven successful time and again throughout history. None of them involve "can't-miss trading secrets" handed down by ancient shamans, "triple secret for-your-eyes-only" market formulas or get-rich-quick investment newsletters. I hate to bust your bubble, but that's all nonsense.

Let's be sensible about this. Suppose you stumbled upon a foolproof way to guarantee yourself enormous profits in the stock market with no risk at all. Would you:

A.   Keep it to yourself, your family, and maybe a few close friends so you can all become obscenely wealthy?

B.   Sell it to anyone with a credit card for the low, low price of $19.95 per month,* so they can all get wealthy?

The next time you receive a solicitation by mail or television for one of these ridiculous can't-miss schemes, ask yourself a simple question. "If this thing is so great, why are they letting little old me in on it instead of simply making piles of money with it?"

The point is: there are no secret formulas, magic charms, or ancient incantations for becoming a Great Investor. In fact, achieving investment success is much simpler than that. Since I'm absolutely sure the suspense is killing you, I'll share the five elements with you.

They are:

1.   **Great Investors don't follow the herd.**

2.   **Great Investors know themselves and have mastered "risk ignorance".**

3.   **Great Investors define their long-term objectives and invest accordingly.**

4.   **Great Investors ignore short term noise.**

5.   **Great Investors understand the 5 Immutable Laws of the Markets**.

There. Feel better? Let's explore each one of these a little deeper.

---

*   Plus, if you act now, we'll include this potato slicer at no additional charge.

Chapter Summary

♦ There are only three financial goals in life, and accepting this will help simplify the task you have before you.

♦ Assuming you have a reasonable degree of common sense, anyone can become a Great Investor.

♦ Accomplishing your financial goals can be simpler than you may think, if you can just embrace the basic elements that time and experience have proven to be true for countless Great Investors before you.

One hundred thousand lemmings can't be wrong.

—*Graffito*

11

Great Investors Don't Follow the Herd

Now, on the surface, you might be tempted to resist this basic tenet of successful investing. Let me clarify it a bit. When I refer to "the herd," I am referring specifically to:

♦ The vast majority of unguided do-it-yourself investors relying on one another for investment advice. They include your neighbor, the guy at the water cooler, your boss, the paperboy, and your spouse's first cousin twice removed who has "connections." We will refer to these folks as "the great unwashed."

♦ The media, for reasons that, if they aren't already, will become apparent shortly.

♦ Anyone who doesn't invest other people's money as their chosen profession.

The most basic and obvious reasons to ignore the actions of unguided investors should be obvious. First, they typically have no personal interest in or knowledge of your personal goals and objectives. Second, you would only follow the actions of others because you believe they have better insight or better information than you. History shows us time and again this is most certainly not the case.

Unguided investors have historically done the exact opposite of what *rational* investors would do, often with disastrous results. When average investors see their neighbors, co-workers, and others riding a bull market or a particular rising investment, a social consensus is formed. A "herd mentality" develops. Goals and rational thinking go out the window and emotions take over. History is a great teacher of what happens to investors in these instances.

Here are a few poignant examples to demonstrate what I mean by the average unguided investor doing the opposite of what sane rational investors should do:

Tulip Mania

In 1559, Conrad Guestner brought the first tulip bulbs from Constantinople to Holland and Germany, and people fell in love with them. Soon tulip bulbs became a status symbol for the wealthy—because they were beautiful and hard to get.

Although early buyers were people who truly prized the lovely flowers, later buyers were merely in it for the money. It didn't take long for speculators to get involved. By 1634, the rage for owning tulips had spread to the middle classes of Dutch society. Merchants and shopkeepers began to vie with one another for single tulip bulbs.

At the height of tulip mania in 1635, a single tulip bulb was sold for:

4 tons of wheat	8 tons of rye	4 tons of beer
12 sheep	4 oxen	8 pigs
2 tons of butter	1,000 pounds of cheese	1 suit of clothes
1 bed	1 silver drinking cup	2 casks of wine

People from all walks of life liquidated their homes and real estate at incredibly low prices in order to speculate in tulip trading. But in 1636, some began to liquidate their tulip holdings. Tulip prices began to weaken, slowly at first, and then rapidly. Confidence was soon destroyed, and panic seized the market. Within six weeks, tulip prices crashed by 90%.

Defaults on contracts and liens on owners were widespread. Tulip prices soon plunged to less than the present equivalent of a dollar each. Imagine having bought a tulip for $76,000, only to discover six weeks later that it was now worth less than one dollar.

The Great Crash of 1929

After World War I, the United States experienced an economic boom unlike any other in its history. Ford, General Electric, and RCA led the industrial revolution, and America prospered. In 1926, the Dow Jones Industrial Average stood at 100. By mid-1929, it was at 350, largely driven by an influx of individual investors who were allowed to purchase stock on credit. $100 dollars would buy you $1,000 dollars worth of stock. Investors mortgaged their homes to buy more. In September of 1929, the house of cards collapsed. Wall Street called due all its loans, and thousands upon thousands of average investors were completely wiped out. America sunk into the Great Depression.

"There's Gold in Them Thar Hills"

In 1974, gold sold for roughly $42 an ounce. Other than a few speculative spikes in buying, investors generally treated gold like it was radioactive and wanted nothing to do with it. By 1980, it had reached $850 an ounce and people couldn't buy enough of it at this price. Investor purchases of gold skyrocketed. By 1985, gold had fallen to $284 an ounce and investor purchases had again declined to historical levels. In early 2008, as gold rocketed past $900 an ounce, unguided investors couldn't buy enough of it.

The Internet Bubble

In 1993, the Internet revolution was born. Hundreds of companies promising to change the world went public and investors couldn't get enough of them. In May of 1999, one internet company *with no earnings at all* was worth more than Delta Airlines, US Air, and United Airlines combined.

Stocks were discussed at the water cooler and purchased immediately thereafter by anyone in earshot. Gardeners, janitors, and doormen suddenly became expert stock pickers.

On many days, the total number of shares of particular stocks traded many times over, meaning that investors were simply trading the same stock with each other at higher and higher prices.[*]

In 2000, the bubble popped. Thousands of investors saw their hard earned savings evaporate in a few short months. Hundreds of billions of dollars simply disappeared into thin air virtually overnight.

History—both ancient and current—is full of examples of unguided investors following supposedly smarter investors to their ruin. Let's look at a current day example.

Chasing Yesterday's Winners

From January 1984 through December 2003, the average stock mutual fund investor earned a paltry 3.51% compounded annually. But, the stock market (as measured by the S&P 500) returned 12.98%[32]

Returns Among U.S. Equity Mutual Fund Investors
1984 – 2003

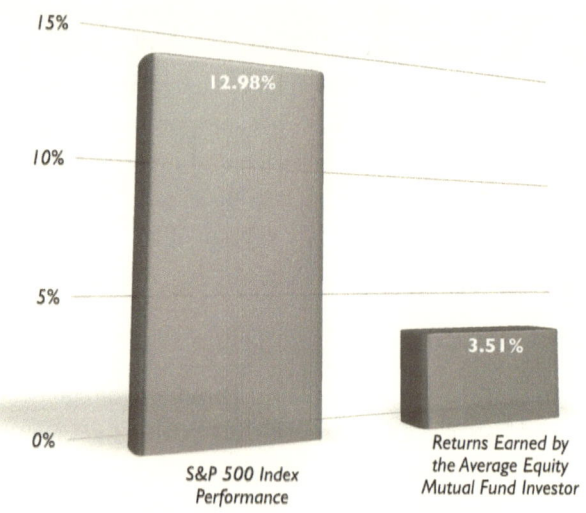

Dalbar. Quantitative Analysis of Investor Behavior update, 2003

---

[*] This is commonly known as the "Greater Fool" investment strategy. I recommend that you avoid it at all cost.

The primary reason for this dismal performance? Investors tend to sell investments that are underperforming and buy investments that have performed well in the recent past. Yale Professor Owen Lamont and the University of Chicago's Andrea Frazzini studied mutual fund investors' behavior from 1980–2003. They concluded the following:

> *"Our main result is that, on average, retail investors direct their money to funds which invest in stocks that have low future returns. To achieve high returns, it is best to do the opposite of these investors. We calculate that mutual fund investors experience total returns that are significantly lower due to their reallocations (authors note: chasing yesterday's winners). Therefore, mutual fund investors are "dumb" in the sense that their reallocations reduce their wealth on average. We call this predictability the "dumb money" effect."* [33] *

Here's more specific evidence of this unfortunate trait. Morningstar, the mutual fund research firm, evaluated 199 no-load mutual funds (a favorite investment for unguided investors) from 1989–1994. The average annual return for the 199 funds for that period was 12.01%. Given that the average no-load mutual fund investor holds funds for only 21 months, the individual owners of those same funds received a return of just 2.02% for their various periods of ownership. Either chasing hot managers or trying to time the market turned a potential 12% return into 2%.[34]

Now, a fact that hopefully strikes you as glaringly obvious apparently eludes most people:

You cannot recapture the returns of yesterday's hot investments. Those returns belong to someone else. They are a part of history, and there's nothing you can do about it.

If you understand this simple fact, consider yourself smarter than the herd. We know that today's hot performing investments historically have not been tomorrow's hot performing investments. And yet, investors continue this

---

*   If you are offended by the term "dumb money", it's probably because you see yourself in this club. Sorry, the truth can sometimes be painful.

malignant pattern of self-abuse. In the previous example, an investor who naively invested in the S&P 500 index and went to sleep for 19 years did three times better than those who actively tried to beat the markets through chasing yesterday's winners, market timing, and other losing tactics. Following the herd is simply not the path to investment success. In the words of one of Wall Street's great early investors, Bernard Baruch, "If you see a bandwagon, it's too late."

Let's look at one particular investor—Jack Sprat. Jack is 63 and looking forward to retirement. He grew up in a middle-class household and learned most of what he knows about investing from his parents, who lost most of their savings in the Depression. Jack has kept his savings in a passbook savings account and, with his pension from work, is looking forward to a moderately comfortable retirement.

> *It's the summer of 1987. Jack has watched the Dow Jones Average's meteoric rise from 838 in 1980 to 2400 in June of 1987—roughly tripling its value. Still he has resisted the temptation to invest, since he knows from his upbringing that stocks are a form of financial poison. Finally, he can wait no longer. The markets are going to the moon without him.*
>
> *So, he dips into his savings account and buys a stock mutual fund that mimics the S&P 500 in July. Things look rosy, and Jack enjoys watching his monthly statements as the value of his account increases. Then, October 19, 1987 rolls around. In one day, Jack's account declines by more than 20%. He sells the next day, kicks himself repeatedly for his foolish speculation, and retires to his La-Z-Boy© to lick his wounds.* *
>
> *Fast forward to 1998. Ten years have passed since Jack's disastrous foray into the stock market. The Dow Jones stands at 8,900, more than four times its value since Jack's last visit. In ten years! Jack sees that the markets are again on a tear. There's no end in sight, and he cannot resist the temptation to get his share. On the advice of the financial newscasters, Jack buys a technology stock because they are bulletproof. He is delighted by the performance, and buys more. And*

---

* By the way, if Jack had simply stayed put, his account would have roughly been even by February of 1988, a mere five months later. But, I digress.

more. Then, in March of 2000, a long slow, painful decline begins, and Jack rides his stock all the way to the bottom. He sells his shares for one-tenth of what he paid and vows again to never invest in the stock market.

Had enough? So why do so many investors make such terribly timed decisions by chasing yesterday's winners?

There are two reasons, and they are both in your head. The first is what we refer to as the cycle of market emotions. Here's how it works. When the prices of investments are declining, emotions run high. Fear and alarm take over. When prices are rising, elation and optimism are rampant.

Cycle of Market Emotions

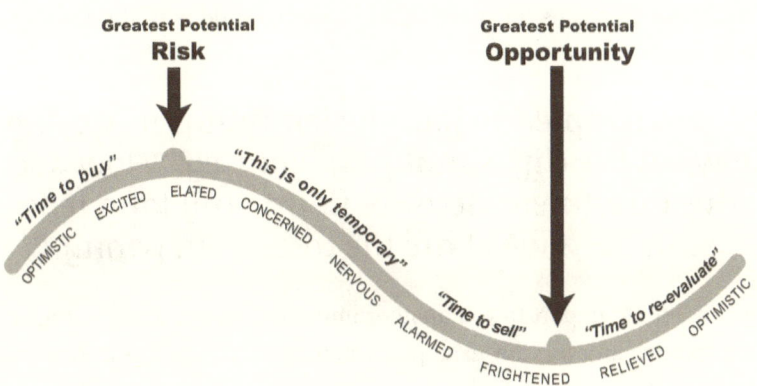

The second reason is closely related to the first. It's called "anchoring." Anchoring refers to the tendency of most investors to think that the future will pretty much be like the recent past. This explains how investors like Jack always seem to buy high and sell low, and why the vast majority of investors take money out of investments that are performing poorly and put money into investments that have been outperforming. A rational investor, by the way, would do precisely the opposite. This also explains why investors continued to pour money into technology stocks even in early 2000, because they believed that the most recent advances were likely to continue indefinitely.

Note well: This is speculation in its worst form. It is a gamble on future market direction with absolutely no consideration for your long-term goals and objectives.

Let me give you a current day example of anchoring that you might personally be experiencing. If I told you that a reasonable inflation forecast for the coming years was 5%, you would likely tell me I was slightly crazy. Why? Because inflation has been running around 3% for a number of years now and has only recently moved above it. Yet, for the thirty-year period from 1973–2004, the average inflation rate was about 4.5%.[35] See my point? You are wired to believe that the recent past is what the future will look like. If you understand anchoring, it becomes easier to understand how unguided investors have made, and continue to make, poor investment decisions at the worst possible time.

How can you avoid the cycle of market emotions and anchoring? It's simpler than you might think.

First, these gyrations have absolutely nothing to do with the three goals of all Great Investors.

When tempted to join the lemmings marching toward the cliff, simply ask yourself, "How does this investment decision fit into my long term plan, and what are the costs if I'm wrong?"

Second, let me impart to you another important lesson to becoming a Great Investor through an everyday example. You may refer to this as the *supermarket investing strategy.*

Suppose you went to the supermarket today to buy a can of baked beans. You note that a can of baked beans costs $2.50. How many cans would you buy? You may decide to buy none, as baked beans seem expensive today. Let's assume you go back next week, and you notice that baked beans are now on sale: 3 cans for $3.00. How many cans would you buy? You'd stock up, right? This appears to be perfectly rational behavior.

Why is it that when it comes to our hard-earned investment dollars, so many of us do exactly the opposite and behave irrationally? What is so difficult about buying the stuff that's on sale and ignoring the stuff that's overpriced? If most investors would apply this supermarket investing strategy to their investment portfolios, their results would be far superior to those they have likely experienced in the past. Care for some proof that the way you shop should be the way you invest?

In another Morningstar study covering the period from 1987–1994, analysts compared mutual fund returns each year with the returns for the next one, two, and three years. They found that funds from the three least popular equity categories (those funds effectively "on sale") outperformed funds from the three most popular equity categories (those most popular with unguided investors) *22 out of 24 times.*[36] I suggest you use this supermarket analogy the next time you are presented with an investment opportunity that is accompanied by the phrase "this is what everyone is buying."

Finally, let's apply a little rational thinking. Here's where math becomes your ally.[*] It's called "Reversion to the Mean." It means, generally speaking, that markets go through cycles of expansion and contraction. When you smooth these cycles out over time, the markets have tended to produce average returns—over the long-haul—that are reasonably consistent. For instance, between 1926 and 2002, the average annual return on the S&P 500 was about 10.2%.

Now, let's assume that, over longer periods of time, these are reasonable average expectations for the market. What might we conclude about the future when recent yearly returns look like this?

YEAR	S&P 500 Return
1995	+37.5%
1996	+22.9%
1997	+33.4%
1998	+28.5%
1999	+21.0%

Of course, hindsight is a great tool, but we might conclude that the likelihood of the markets continuing this stratospheric rise probably decreases with each passing day.

---

[*]   I have promised not to bombard you with complicated graphs, charts, and principles, but this is one you should know.

Markets do not go up indefinitely. They never have, and never will.*

Let's look at what the next four years delivered:

YEAR	S&P 500 Return
2000	-9.1%
2001	-11.8%
2002	-22.1%
2003	+28.6%

Interestingly enough, if you average the S&P 500's return from 1995–2003, you get 11.3%—about the long-term historical average.[37] The markets do not always revert to the mean this neatly or conveniently, but it's a useful point to remember as you try and avoid projecting the recent past into the future.

In summary, following the herd will likely lead to you stepping in the unpleasant mess left by those in front of you.

---

*   Later, we'll describe why this is a good thing.

Chapter Summary

♦ Doing what everyone else is doing presumes they are smarter than you. They aren't. Throughout investment history, the actions of the masses have done much more harm to them than good. In order to be successful, you must resist the temptation to simply follow along.

♦ Yesterday's winners are rarely tomorrow's winners.

♦ Try and apply the way you shop at the supermarket to your investment philosophy. You'll eat better and sleep better.

Knowledge comes, but wisdom lingers.

—Alfred Lord Tennyson

12

Great Investors Know Themselves

When it comes to investing, particularly for retirement, most people simply aren't "self-aware." This means they have no idea why they make the decisions they do, they just do. Witness:

♦ In mid-2003, investors were pouring money into bond funds instead of stock funds—even though interest rates had fallen to less than nothing after inflation and taxes—while the stock market was beginning to show signs of life.

♦ In late 1999, investor purchases of technology mutual funds reached their peak. In March of 2000, the Internet bubble cracked. Between January 2000 and March 2001, more than $1 trillion in investor wealth was wiped out.

♦ Large financial institutions use a series of indicators to tell them when markets are approaching a peak. One of their key indicators is driven by buying activity of individual investors, who have consistently increased their stock purchases right before major market declines.

♦ A recent study of 66,000 customers of a major discount broker compared their returns to the returns of the overall market. Investors who traded frequently earned just 11.4%, considerably below the markets return of 17.9% for the same period.[38]

The fields of Psychology and Finance have historically been about as far apart as two academic pursuits can be. Only recently have the two been considered together as researchers have been trying to understand what drives investors to make such consistently terrible investment decisions.

The science of "Behavioral Finance" seeks to understand the mental properties driving your investment decisions. In the interest of not boring you to distraction with reams of scientific data, I'll cut to the heart of what the research has revealed:

Being a Great Investor isn't about knowing the markets—it's about knowing yourself.

When I was studying Behavioral Psychology at the University of Maryland, we trained birds—pigeons, to be exact. At the time, I recall questioning whether my student loan dollars were being utilized effectively, but the experience taught me something very important about behavior.

In order to understand how behavior was learned, we would place pigeons in a box, which had several small levers on one wall. When the pigeon pecked the correct lever, it received a small reward of pigeon food. Other studies were performed where selecting the wrong lever resulted in a small electrical shock—not lethal—but just enough to get the birds attention. So they learned the lesson: pick the right lever, get fed; pick the wrong lever, and get an unpleasant wake up call. After too many choices with the wrong lever, the pigeon would simply lose interest in eating. Sounding a little like your past investment experience?

People and pigeons have this in common: they learn from their experiences. Many of today's seniors who lived through the Great Depression still keep their entire investment savings in US Government bonds and CDs—over 75 years later. Folks who "pulled" the Great Internet lever in the late 1990s are still suffering from the shock they received. They have sworn never again to buy the stock of a company ending in the suffix "dot com." With these kinds of experiences, it is no wonder that most Americans are paralyzed when trying to make sound investment decisions.

This chapter is designed to give you a fundamental understanding of why you think like you do when it comes to investing and to offer you a way to pick the right levers to get the rewards you so richly deserve for retirement.

Two Brains Are Better Than One

Where investment decisions get made

Your brain has two distinct operating units—the left side and the right side.* The left side of your brain processes data. It's where logic, analysis, and precision live. Let's call it the "hard stuff." It's where *thinking* takes place.

Conversely, the right side of your brain is where the "soft stuff" lives—intuition, emotion, perception, that sort of thing. It's where *feeling* takes place. Here's a visual illustration of each side of your brain and its function:

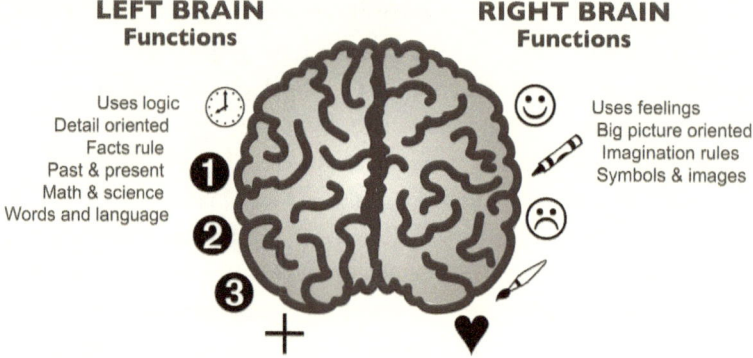

LEFT BRAIN
Functions

Uses logic
Detail oriented
Facts rule
Past & present
Math & science
Words and language

RIGHT BRAIN
Functions

Uses feelings
Big picture oriented
Imagination rules
Symbols & images

Now, evaluate the following conversation and tell me if you can determine where many investment decisions get made:

> *Broker: "As you can plainly see from this chart, the XYZ fund has had a standard deviation of 14.2 and a total return of 20 basis points better than the S&P 500 index for the last 64 years. Therefore, you should buy it in your retirement account."*

> *Investor: "Okay, if I buy it, will I lose all my money? How will I pay my bills then?"*

---

* You have undoubtedly heard the expression "left brain/right brain"—that's what it means.

Here is our first lesson:

Wall Street sells facts to the left side of our brain.

You see, Wall Street has historically represented its investment advice to the investing public through a confusing array of charts, graphs, and complicated formulas. People haven't been trained to understand how they *feel* about their investment decisions. Instead, we have been conditioned to make investment decisions based on what these charts, graphs, and formulas reflect. This requires us to recognize a truth that is all too easy to miss:

Investment decisions are more emotional decisions than analytical ones. Good or bad, they are often driven by a mixture of hope, faith, greed, and fear—not by a bunch of numbers on a chart.

You see, when you are confronted with overwhelming charts, data, and confusing mathematics, you fall back on thousands of years of evolution to make decisions intuitively—without formal analysis. Your brain doesn't work like a computer. Instead, it processes information through a series of shortcuts and emotional filters to shorten the analysis time. It asks questions like:

Is this going to hurt me or help me?
Will I be okay?

This is amplified by the fact that financial decisions about retirement are *emotional* and cause stress. The more stress, the more your brain relies on basic perception and intuition—and less on facts and logic—for decisions. It is very difficult to apply logic when the question is, "will I outlive my money?"

Since we're talking about decisions that will affect your standard of living for the rest of your life, one might conclude that you rely more on feeling than on fact. Wall Street has largely missed this simple concept:

> *People make their investment decisions based on what they want an investment to do for them in retirement, not based on what it's done, mathematically, in the past.*

Let me give you an example of how your right-brain controls these decisions. A recent study evaluated the way investors respond to mutual fund advertising.[39] Participants were shown a number of ads for hypothetical mutual funds and were asked to predict the future returns and risks of each fund. The ads contained exactly the same information, but different amounts of "emotional" content—such as graphic images, slogans, and marketing appeals. Each fund had a numerical value in its name, such as the EURO 100 or ASIA 500.

Care to guess the results of the study? It found that test participants consistently predicted higher returns for funds with more emotionally appealing ads and for funds with higher numeric values in their names. Same financial data—just prettier, more emotionally appealing pictures.

If investors perceive that an investment is a good one, they tend to be more comfortable investing in it. Think back to the last major investment decision you made. How did you feel? Were you a little nervous? Palms sweaty? Perhaps a bit reluctant? Uncertain? These are *normal* reactions, because you are under stress. They are emotional reactions. Logic and reason rarely cause sweaty palms.

The point here is not to try and turn you into some kind of left-brain junkie for charts and graphs so you can make dispassionate, logical decisions. That's a fool's errand. You will continue to make investment decisions on the right side of your brain, because we are *all* wired that way. I simply wish to raise your awareness for how you are wired so you can make good decisions based on understanding your feelings and understanding the facts. By developing a mental checklist, you can develop more comfort with your decision-making process.

I created a simple scorecard that can help you exercise both sides of your brain when making investment decisions. It's designed to have you ask yourself the right questions to illuminate both the right and left-brain activity necessary to make sound investment decisions. Much of the content of this scorecard will be more useful to you as you continue through this book. You'll be able to answer the questions more comfortably as you go along, so bookmark the page for easy reference.

Chapter Summary

♦ Understand that investment decisions are emotional ones and consist of a mixture of hope, faith, greed, and fear.

♦ Use both sides of your brain so you can greatly increase your chances of making sound investment decisions.

The Great Investors Facts and Feelings Scorecard

1. **How do I feel about the data that's been presented on this decision? The history, the charts, graphs, or other financial information I have before me?**
   a. I understand it completely
   b. I understand most of it
   c. I understand some of it
   d. I'm confused by it

2. **Do I have enough information to comfortably assess this investment?**
   a. Yes
   b. No
   c. I'm not sure

3. **Do I fully understand the risks of making this investment for my retirement needs?**
   a. Yes
   b. No

4. **Overall, am I comfortable with the risks I see in this investment?**
   a. Yes
   b. No

5. **Does this investment make sense to me logically? Do I feel good about it?**
   a. Yes
   b. No

6. **Why am I making this investment decision?**
   a. I'll feel like I'm missing out on an opportunity if I don't
   b. It feels like the right thing to do for what I want to accomplish in retirement.
   c. I have to do something with the money – this seems okay

7. **If this investment declines 10% within one year of my purchase I will:**
   a. Feel as if I made a big mistake by buying it
   b. Be concerned, but probably hold on to it
   c. I'll be disappointed, but still confident it will accomplish what I need

8. **The person recommending this investment:**
   a. Is someone I trust who has professional experience in providing advice
   b. Is my neighbor or co-worker, who has done really well investing
   c. Is a friend of the family
   d. Is me – I'm doing it all myself, but I'm doing my homework

9. **I'm making this decision because this investment:**
   a. Fits well within my overall retirement goals and objectives
   b. Is matched to a specific goal I have
   c. Has a great track record

10. **Based on what I know, how do I feel about this investment decision?**
    a. Supremely confident
    b. Somewhat confident
    c. A little nervous
    d. Not confident at all

	A	B	C	D	Your Score
1.	5	3	1	0	_____
2.	5	0	0	-	_____
3.	5	0	-	-	_____
4.	5	0	-	-	_____
5.	5	0	-	-	_____
6.	1	5	0	-	_____
7.	0	3	5	-	_____
8.	5	0	0	2	_____
9.	5	5	1	-	_____
10.	5	3	2	0	_____
				Your Total Score:	_____

26 – 50: You are in pretty good shape. You've assessed the risks of this investment and matched it up to your goals. You understand the information you need to make a reasonable decision.

10-25: You need to do some more homework. You haven't become comfortable enough with this investment decision to make it and sleep well at night. It may still be a good choice, but you need

0-10: Forget it. You are investing by accident. Start over at the beginning.

Ignorance is voluntary misfortune.

—Nicholas Lang

13

Mastering your own risk ignorance

An essential element of knowing yourself as a Great Investor means understanding your tolerance for risk. Quite simply, too many of us are "risk ignorant", meaning we have no idea how to quantify how much or little risk we can comfortably stand in many aspects of our lives.

In a recent New York Times article, Jeffrey Kluger holds forth on the subject of risk in general. He notes that we fret over the bird flu, which has killed precisely zero people in the US, but we must be dragged to the doctor to get vaccinated against the common flu, which presently kills 36,000 Americans each year. He further muses that we wring our hands over mad cow disease which might, though likely isn't, in our cheeseburger; yet we worry far less about the cholesterol that contributes to heart disease, which kills 700,000 of us annually.

Yahoo® Finance columnist Robert Kiyosaki notes amusingly that in 2003, there were 17,732 murders and only *one* death by shark attack. By contrast, there were 685,000 deaths by heart attack and 44,000 deaths by automobile accident—eclipsing those caused either by sharks or by murderers. Despite these statistics, people are more afraid of sharks and murderers than of driving their car up to the fast food window and super-sizing that order of fries. It makes no sense.*

The message here is that too often we worry about the wrong things. That's certainly clear when we try to assess our tolerance for investment risk. By not understanding and mastering what it means to us personally, we will only be financially successful by accident.

"But," you protest, "taking risks with my money makes my palms sweat. It makes me queasy. It keeps me up at night." So, here's a question:

*Which condition makes you so uncomfortable: what you **do** know about investment risk, or what you **don't**?*

Most people are made uncomfortable by what they *don't* know. There is hope, however. You can have a rational response to risk if you are willing to educate yourself. We will seek to illuminate some of those fears, explain them, and prove that risk can be our friend after all—and not our enemy.

Why Risk Evokes Fear

Risk lives in your right (emotional) brain, and it is fairly impervious to reason and logic. To a purely rational investor, the risk of loss and the possibility of gain should be exactly equal, but they are not. Investors tend to place twice as much importance on avoiding losses. For example, to accept a 50% chance of losing $100, most people will insist on having a 50% chance of winning $200. Why? Because regret is naturally a stronger emotion than pride.

People generally avoid actions that cause regret, and seek actions that cause pride. The emotional pain that comes from making a decision that turns out badly is stronger than the emotional joy that comes from a decision that turns out well. Remember our story about Jack Sprat? Jack bought, but didn't sell as his investment continued to decline. The pain of regret was simply too great.†

---

*   Note that if you don't go in the ocean, your odds of dying from a shark attack drop even further: to approximately zero.

†   For those of you clinging to shares of Internet stocks in the hope that they will someday return to their former glory…well, you get the point.

Another example may help explain this. Here's a test that was given to hundreds of subjects, see what you would do:

> *You are forced to flip a coin. If you lose the coin toss, you lose $100. If you win the coin toss, you lose nothing. If you choose, you can pay $50 to avoid flipping the coin.*

If you are like most people, you would pay the $50. Why?

We will often take great risks to avoid the pain of regret or financial loss. Many people believe they are avoiding the pain of regret, due to financial loss, by putting their investment dollars into "safe" investments like CDs and money market accounts. After all, the opposite of "risky" is "safe," right? Wrong. I'll prove it to you.

Throughout history, and more specifically since the Depression, people have been taught that safety means getting your money back and risk means potentially losing it. But, this isn't a correct statement. The terms 'risky' and 'safe' are not opposites.

> *Let's say it's 1976. You have a dollar. You don't think you'll need it for the next twenty-five years or so. You have two choices where to put it— you can put it in a vault in your basement where it will be "safe," or you can invest it in the S&P 500 index of stocks. You know that stocks are "risky" and your vault is "safe," so you put that dollar in your vault. As you read the paper, you mentally note that the cost of a stamp today is 13 cents, which means your dollar would buy you about seven stamps.*
>
> *It's now 2003. You need to use that dollar, because you need to buy seven stamps. You go to the vault, open it up, and behold! Your dollar is there, safe and sound as you had predicted. You take your dollar down to the post office to buy some stamps, and you receive a nasty surprise: that dollar will buy just two stamps today—not the seven it would have bought you in 1976.*

In this case, you suffered what is known as *purchasing power risk*. That same "safe" dollar now buys five less stamps because the cost of stamps rose in price by 280% over 29 years, eventually costing 37 cents.

We often confuse "safety" with "certainty," and they are two very different things. *Safe* is defined as "unlikely to cause or result in harm, injury, or damage". *Certain* is defined as "having no doubts about something."

Did we harm ourselves by storing the dollar in the vault? We were depending on that dollar to buy us seven stamps. Perhaps that means our utility company will not receive our payment, or that a family member will not receive our birthday card. That dollar bill was certainly still there, though ultimately, we could not use it to maintain the quality of life we had anticipated when we set it aside.

Let's look at what would have happened had we chosen the "risky" strategy of buying stocks. If we had invested our dollar in the S&P 500 index of stocks in 1976 and went to the market to claim our dollar in 2003, we would have roughly $6.50 (after taxes and inflation) in our pocket. That amount buys us over 17 stamps. Certainly, the value of our dollar in the S&P 500 went up and down over the years. Since we didn't need it right away, time was on our side.

The moral of the story is that every single investment on Earth—including putting your money under your mattress—has some form of risk to it.

There is no such thing as a risk-free investment.

Whether we purchase government bonds, CDs, or bury our money in the backyard, it may still be there years later. As we learned earlier, though, a dollar today is not worth a dollar tomorrow. Everyone faces inflation (aka purchasing power) risk. Since we continually pay higher prices for the items we use in everyday life, over time we continually need more money just to maintain the same quality of life that we enjoy today. If our dollar had earned us an extra ten cents each year, we could have bought those seven stamps and more.

The longer you plan to be alive, the more insidious and dangerous purchasing power risk becomes. The only way to combat it is to select investments that will grow faster than inflation and your tax bill. The key for Great Investors is to determine the level of risk they can comfortably stand, and how much short-term fluctuation they can tolerate in the value of their investment portfolio.

It's critically important to understand this concept of loss of purchasing power. As noted earlier, in the early 1970s the average male retired at 65 and died around 72. His retirement money only needed to stretch out over seven years. Purchasing power risk was a smaller factor in this shorter time period, and people had much less risk of outliving their savings or retirement income.

Today, folks are retiring earlier and living much, much longer. As we learned earlier, most of us can expect to live another thirty to forty years after we retire.

Purchasing power risk becomes a major risk. Above all, we need to ensure that we don't outlive our income or compromise our living standard. Here's the estimated cost of a few typical items in the future, assuming a 4% inflation rate:

Estimated Costs of Typical Items

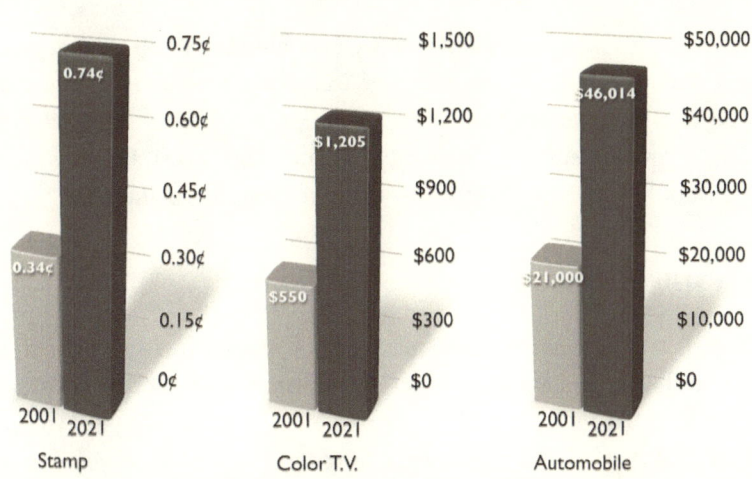

Based on an average annual inflation rate of 4%.

One last point about inflation:

Relying on one big "inflation" number doesn't truly reflect the danger that purchasing power risk presents to your everyday lifestyle.

For example, most people rely on the Consumer Price Index (CPI) as the measure of overall inflation. From September 1986 to September 2006, the CPI rose 84.3%. During the same time period, however, college tuition jumped a staggering 289.5%. The cost of hospital services soared up an additional 280%. Prescription drug costs hiked up 177.6%. The cost of energy: 131.9%.[40]

Simply saying that "inflation rose 4% last year" may mean your grocery bill went from $100 to $104, but your heating bill, your medical care costs, and Junior's tuition rose by so much more.

Other Types of Risk

Now that we've explored and educated ourselves about purchasing power risk, let's look at the other types of risk that affect all investments in one way or another.*

Specific Risk

This refers to the risk you inherit when you decide to put all your eggs in one basket. Former shareholders of Enron or WorldCom are painfully familiar with this type of risk. Specific risk refers to things that happen specifically to a company, a government, or other entity in which you invest. Owning too much of one particular investment subjects you to too much specific risk.

Market risk

Market risk refers to the natural tendency of overall investment markets to advance and decline. Markets generally advance and decline in a cyclical fashion in relation to the overall economic environment. As such, you inherit the likelihood that, with a moderate to long-term outlook (five years or more), you will probably experience some market risk. It is important to become comfortable with the concept of market risk because it is also the great reward for those who understand it.

Interest rate risk

Interest rate risk is concerned with the danger that your investment will lose value because it has a fixed rate of return that will not change as interest rates rise. Many investors fail to consider this type of risk as a factor when putting savings into fixed rate investments such as bank certificates of deposit, or CDs.

For example, let's say you want to invest $10,000 into a one-year certificate of deposit that pays 5% interest annually. A week later, interest rates rise a whole percentage point. That may not seem like a lot to you, but over time, a single percentage point can have a major impact on the amount of money you can save. Left to compound for 10 years, $10,000 invested at 5% will grow to

---

* Don't get discouraged by all this discussion of risk, because we will also shortly see how to defeat these risks quite effectively.

$16,289. The same amount, invested at 6% will reach $17,908 over the same time period. That's $1,619 more.

Your problem is this: your investment will continue to pay 5%, but because you've committed to hold the investment until it matures, you can't take advantage of the higher interest rate without facing penalties or surrender charges. Interest rate risk is the reason you want to make sure that you balance fixed rate investments with investments whose return can keep up with inflation.

Liquidity risk

Liquidity risk refers to the risk you inherit when you purchase an investment that may not provide access to your funds when needed. A typical example is a certificate of deposit, which may have a penalty for early withdrawal should you need the funds prior to a stated period of time. Another example would be real estate, which tends to be fairly illiquid. This risk can generally be avoided by ensuring that adequate emergency reserves are set aside in a liquid investment such as a money market account.

Now you have a general understanding of risk in its different forms. This understanding will be powerful as you continue toward becoming a Great Investor. Let's explore how to minimize these risks and turn them to our advantage.

For the moment, accept the notion that you cannot eliminate risk completely. (In fact, you wouldn't want to, as you'll learn in Chapter 16.) If you cannot eliminate it, how can you minimize it?

There are three essential principles which will allow you to harness risk and use it to your advantage:

Principle #1: Diversification

Diversification simply means spreading your investment dollars across different types of investments. Investment professionals will often refer to diversification as "asset allocation"—appropriately allocating your dollars across different types of assets to minimize your risk while maximizing your potential return. Examples of some asset classes are:

♦   Small Stocks

♦   Large Stocks

♦   International Stocks

♦   Bonds

♦   Real estate

♦   Cash

How does diversification work? History teaches us that investments behave differently from each other over time. When some go up, others go down. And so on. In general terms, bonds and stocks have historically (over the long term) moved in opposite directions. That is, when stock values are going down, bond values tend to go up, and vice versa. By owning both stocks and bonds, you minimize the risks of one by owning the other as well. By spreading your investment dollars across different types of investments, you take advantage of this powerful tool. This provides the wonderful benefit of reducing your risk while providing you with the opportunity for greater returns over time.

We'll cover this in more detail later, but here is a visual example of effective diversification.

Effective vs. Ineffective Diversification

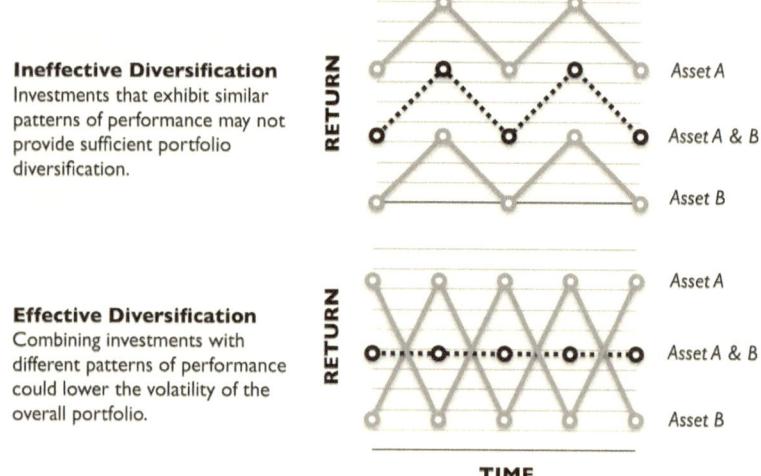

Ineffective Diversification
Investments that exhibit similar patterns of performance may not provide sufficient portfolio diversification.

RETURN

Asset A

Asset A & B

Asset B

Effective Diversification
Combining investments with different patterns of performance could lower the volatility of the overall portfolio.

RETURN

Asset A

Asset A & B

Asset B

TIME

92

Note that owning the dotted line with effective diversification much smoother. If you choose not to diversify, you are essentially betting that you will not incur one of the various forms of risk. The principle of diversification accepts that the various forms of risks are real and cannot be eliminated, but can be minimized and in fact turned to your advantage.

Principle #2: Fluctuation Does Not Equal Loss

Let's say you buy a mutual fund for $15.00 a share. You look in the paper a week later and notice the share price is now $14.50. (Congratulations—you've now experienced Market Risk.) How do you respond?

A. I lost 50 cents. I'm ruined. I'm selling.

B. My investment has declined. Oh well, I'll wait for it to come back because I know from my training as a Great Investor that investments go up and down over time.

C. Oh, goody. Shares of my fund are cheaper now. That means they are effectively on sale. I'll buy some more.

If you answered "A," I'm sorry to inform you that you are still risk ignorant. Go back and read the entire book again as penance.

If you answered "B" or C," you are on your way to becoming a Great Investor.

You see, you haven't "lost" anything until you actually panic and sell. Most investments fluctuate in value, and they fluctuate in proportion to their risk and their potential for reward.

A great example of this principle occurred fairly recently in our history. The date was October 19, 1987. Black Monday, as it was called. The Dow Jones Industrial Average fell 22% in just one day. If you owned the basket of stocks that made up the Dow Jones Industrials, and you sold them on Tuesday morning, you indeed lost 22%. If you held on to your investment and didn't panic, your portfolio recovered to its October 18th ("pre-crash") value by the end of 1987—just three months later.

Remember, fluctuation does not equal loss. The only way to guarantee a loss is to panic and sell.

Principle #3: Know Your Tolerance For Risk

Let's assume I built three diversified portfolios, and I mapped their historical risk and return. Here's what it might look like:

Hypothetical Portfolio Risk and Return Examples

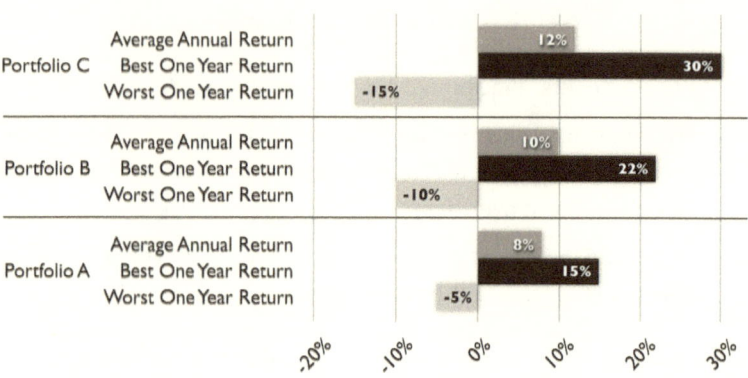

You might say, "I can live with Portfolio B's historical risk and return, but Portfolio C scares the daylights out of me." While we cannot predict the future results of Portfolio B, we can use its historical characteristics to help select a diversification that meets our needs and gives us some level of predictability and expectation.

These three simple principles can help you master risk and leverage it to your advantage.

The following is a personal <u>Risk Questionnaire</u> you can use to help determine your Risk Profile. In addition to being a handy tool for defining risk, it's a great educational resource to assess your feelings on the subject of risk. This profiling tool should help you quantify your tolerance level for risk and give you a solid foundation for making investment decisions.

Risk Profile Questionnaire

1. **What is your investment horizon — when will you want to use your invested money?**
   a. 3 – 5 years
   b. 6 – 10 years
   c. 11 – 15 years
   d. 16 – 25 years
   e. 25 – 30+ years

2. **What is your most important investment goal?**
   a. I want my investments to be secure. I also need my investments to provide me with income now, or to fund a large expense within the next few years.
   b. I want my investments to grow, but I also want them to provide some income. I am comfortable with moderate market fluctuations.
   c. I am more interested in having my investments grow over the long-term. I am less concerned about income, and I am comfortable with short-term return volatility.
   d. I want long-term aggressive growth and am willing to accept significant short-term market fluctuations.

3. **If you owned an investment that fell by 20% over a short period, what would you do?**
   a. Sell all of the remaining investment
   b. Sell a portion of the remaining investment
   c. Hold the investment and sell nothing
   d. Buy more of the investment

4. **Choose a scenario that best describes the way you monitor your investments.**
   a. I look forward to reviewing my portfolio on a daily basis.
   b. I make it a point to review my portfolio regularly and at least once a month.
   c. I review my portfolio on a quarterly basis.
   d. I only review my portfolio once a year.

5. **Would you invest in a financial product based solely on a brief conversation with a friend, relative, or coworker?**
   a. Absolutely not
   b. Probably not
   c. Probably
   d. Absolutely

6. **Given the four potential outcomes below, how would you invest $10,000?**
   a. The potential of earning between $420 and $3,500 on your investment
   b. The potential of earning up to $5,070, but the risk of losing up to $400
   c. The potential of earning up to $7,070, but the risk of losing up to $1,050
   d. The potential of earning up to $9,050, but the risk of losing up to $1,690

7. **If you could increase your chances of improving your investment returns by taking more risk, would you:**
   a. Be unlikely to take more risks
   b. Be willing to take a little more risk with some of your overall portfolio
   c. Be willing to take a lot more risk with some of your overall portfolio
   d. Be willing to take a lot more risk with your entire overall portfolio

8. **You are offered the opportunity to buy into a franchise for 20% of your gross income. You have a 50% chance of getting back 5 times your investment within 5 years, and a 50% chance of losing half your initial investment. Would you buy into the franchise?**
   a. A. Absolutely not
   b. B. Probably not
   c. C. Probably
   d. D. Absolutely

9. **You just won a cash prize equal to 10% of your annual income. Would you keep the cash or risk losing it all for the possibility of more money? Would you:**
   a. Keep the cash
   b. Risk it all for a 3 out of 4 chance of getting 20%
   c. Risk it all for a 2 out of 4 chance of getting 50%
   d. Risk it all for a 1 out of 4 chance of getting 100%

10. **What type of investor are you?**
    a. You may be reaching retirement or simply prefer to take less risk. Security of capital is your biggest concern.
    b. You may be close to retirement or prefer to take less risk. Security is quite important to you.
    c. You want a balance between growth and security. You are willing to accept some risk for potential higher returns over time.
    d. Growth is important but security is still a factor. You are willing to accept risk for potential higher returns over time.
    e. The growth of your money is your main concern and you plan to be invested for a long time. You are very comfortable with riding out the ups and downs of the market for potential higher long-term results.

	A	B	C	D	E	
1.	0	3	5	8	10	_____
2.	0	2	3	4	-	_____
3.	0	3	4	7	-	_____
4.	0	3	4	7	-	_____
5.	0	2	3	4	-	_____
6.	0	4	6	9	-	_____
7.	0	4	6	9	-	_____
8.	0	2	4	6	-	_____
9.	0	4	6	9	-	_____
10.	0	4	6	8	10	_____

Your Total Score:_____

0-6 CONSERVATIVE: Your investment horizon is short or you may simply prefer to take less risk. Security is your most important concern.

7-22 MODERATE: Your investment horizon is relatively short or you may prefer to take less risk. Security is quite important to you.

23-50 BALANCED: Your investment horizon is long enough to benefit from a balance between growth and security. You are willing to accept some risk for potential higher returns over time.

51-68 GROWTH: Your investment horizon is long enough to benefit from a growth orientation. You will accept risk for potential higher returns over time.

69+ AGGRESSIVE GROWTH: Your investment horizon is long enough to benefit from an aggressive growth orientation. Your main concern is growth of money that will be invested for a long period of time. You are very comfortable riding out the ups and downs in the market for potential higher long-term results

Chapter Summary

♦ Understanding the types of risk you will encounter is an important first step to mastering risk ignorance.

♦ Embracing the three principles of minimizing risk will help you turn risk into a powerful ally.

The person who makes a success of living is the one who sees his goal steadily and aims for it unswervingly. That is dedication.

—Cecil B. DeMille

14

Great Investors Define Their Long-Term Objectives and Invest Accordingly

Congratulations. You are the new trapeze artist in the Great Circus of Life. Today, you're going to walk the tightrope high above the big top while yo-yoing. At the other end awaits great applause, admiration and respect. A stumble would result in failure and pain, as there is no safety net. So, what will you focus your attention on while walking the tightrope—the platform at the end of your journey, or the yo-yo going up and down? Which do you think will provide you with more calm, balance, and ultimately a chance for succeeding, as you traverse the tightrope?

The fact is most unguided investors in the Great Circus of Life focus on the yo-yo, which represents the daily machinations of the investment markets. As a result, many make painful mistakes. Ask many former employees of Enron or WorldCom, who not only counted on these companies for their daily livelihood, but also had their entire 401(k) plan proceeds in company stock. Or, ask any unguided investor who, in 1999, planned to retire in 2002 on his fat technology portfolio. The pain of making mistakes—particularly in the years just preceding or following your retirement, can dramatically affect your ability to regain your balance.

One of the most common mistakes investors make is driven by the gap between their investment decisions and their long-term goals. (At the risk of sounding self-serving, this is where a qualified financial advisor earns his keep.) If you're like most investors, you are typically presented with an investment opportunity based on its benefits such as growth, income, safety, tax deferral, or some combination of these things.

These are certainly accurate characteristics of particular investments. The problem is that most unguided investors do not link these benefits to a particular long-term goal or objective. As a result, most folks typically view an investment as an end, not a means to an end. They do not think of investments as a vehicle to accomplish a specific goal. See if this sounds like a familiar conversation:

Jack:	*I bought this great mutual fund from my 1-800 discount broker today.*
Jill:	*Oh yeah? Why is it great?*
Jack:	*Because it's got a great track record for growth.*
Jill:	*Okay, so why did you buy it?*
Jack:	*For growth, of course.*
Jill:	*No, why did you buy it?*
Jack:	*Because it has beaten the S&P 500 index for 11 years.*
Jill:	*But why did you buy it? To provide a comfortable retirement? To fund your grandchildren's college education? To build a legacy for your family?*
Jack:	*Huh?*

Jack is typical of most unguided investors.* His decision was based on a track record, not a personal goal. Logic would tell you that rational investors consider their entire portfolio and their long-term goals before they make an

---

* Note that Jack receives his investment counsel from a disembodied voice on a toll-free number.

investment decision. Yet—because of the way most of us are wired and because of our past experiences with Wall Street—we focus on features and benefits of an investment instead of what the ultimate purpose of that investment should be. We don't consider the big picture—we make our decisions piece-meal. This is why, when many investors experience a gain, they simply "let it ride" rather than considering the gain in the context of their overall portfolio and making adjustments accordingly.*

Here's another way to think about it. Let's take Jack and Jill in the previous example. We will ask both to put together the same 500-piece jigsaw puzzle. With Jack, we'll just dump the pieces out on the table and let him get to work. With Jill, we'll dump the pieces out, but we'll also give her a picture of the finished puzzle to use. Who do you think will finish first?

Jill, of course,† because Jill has a guide—a picture of what she wants to accomplish. She now looks at the pieces of the puzzle as small pieces of the big picture. She realizes that, by itself, one piece is not particularly helpful. But, by putting the pieces together with a visual image of what she needs to do to be successful, she can successfully complete her goal of finishing the puzzle.

One of the easiest ways to remove investment decisions from the emotional side of your brain and make them dispassionately is to think of investments like you think of other products and services in your life. When you buy any product or service, you are essentially "hiring" it to do a specific job for you. When you purchase a new car, you are "hiring" it to provide safe, worry-free transportation from one place to another. When you employ an accountant, you are "hiring" him or her to provide you with competent tax preparation. When you make an investment purchase, you are "hiring" that investment to accomplish a specific goal for you.

Before you make all your future investment decisions, resist the temptation to just ask yourself, "Is this a good investment decision?" That's where your palms start sweating. Instead, take the following approach. Ask yourself the following questions:

> *If I hire this investment, what will it do for me?*
> *How does this fit into my long-term goals?*

---

* This is not investing, by the way. It's more akin to gambling.

† Jack may in fact give up, which is what many investors without long-term objectives do.

If you can't answer the two questions, don't make the investment.

The greatest investors of our time all make their investment decisions dispassionately. They remove fear and emotion from their decision by focusing on the long-term objective. They hire the right investments to get them there on time with room to spare.

If you disagree with this, here is an alternate strategy. Go to Las Vegas, check into the nicest hotel on the Strip, and gamble your brains out. It's essentially the same thing as unguided investing without a long-term goal, but probably more fun—until you run out of money.

Assuming you agree that goal setting seems to make sense, let's proceed. Goal setting does not require heavy lifting from an intellectual perspective. It simply requires you to identify and commit in writing what's important to you. First, take this short quiz and score yourself on the results:

Which statement best describes your investment goals?

A. Beating the S&P 500 by three points each year.

B. Beating the investment performance of my neighbor, Bill.

C. Wealth accumulation for its own sake.

D. Preparing for a comfortable, worry-free retirement with no compromise in my family's standard of living until we all die.

Hopefully, you chose D. If not, please go back and re-read the entire book again. Slowly.

As I noted above, goal-setting is simply the process of determining what's important to you and why. By defining what's important to you, you'll find that making investment decisions will become easier and much more comfortable.

So, what do we mean by "long-term" goals and objectives? It is sometimes difficult to think about long-term objectives when you initially retire, as your most pressing plans might be cruises, tee times, and resodding the lawn. Think of it in these terms:

Long-term goals and objectives are not about retirement; they're about the rest of your life.

Recall that, on average, you'll be around for a good while. Generally, a good planning horizon is to subtract your age from 100. So, if you're 60 today, we're talking about a forty-year planning horizon. While this may seem unrealistic to you, we're interested in erring on the side of conservatism here. Assuming you do make it, wouldn't you want to ensure that your Three Undeniable Goals are all accomplished?

Say you don't plan to make it past 80 and you spend accordingly, living the life of Riley. Now, fast forward. You're 80, in relatively good health, and you've surprised everyone in your family by your youth and vigor and are remarkably able to wax the chumps at the local golf course! Sadly, though, you're now out of money. Maybe you'll depend on your family, maybe you can make ends meet between Social Security checks, maybe you can scrape together enough to play a round every now and then. Wouldn't it have been better to plan to live a little longer?

How does one go about defining their long-term objectives? Well, you start with the Three Undeniable Goals I mentioned earlier. If you're still having trouble defining your objectives with some specificity, here is an exercise used by George Kinder, co-founder of the Kinder Institute for Life Planning and author of The Seven Stages to Money Maturity. Kinder asks a series of questions[41] to help people determine what's important to them. Get a piece of paper, and write down your answers to the following three questions. Answer them in order, and don't turn to the next question until you've fully answered the previous one.

Question #1:

> *Imagine that you are retiring. You are financially secure, that you have enough money to take care of your needs, now and in the future. How would you live your life? What would you do with the money? Would you change anything? Let your imagination run wild. Don't hold back your dreams. Describe a life that is complete, that is richly yours.*

Question #2:

This time, it's the same scenario as question #1, but you visit your doctor who tells you that you have five to ten years left to live. The good part is that you won't ever feel sick. The bad news is that you will have no notice of the moment of your death. What will you do in the time you have remaining to live? Will you change your life? How?

Question #3:

This time your doctor shocks you with the news that you have only one day left to live. Notice what feelings arise as you confront your very real mortality. Ask yourself: What dreams will be left unfulfilled? What do I wish I had finished or had been? What do I wish I had done? What did I miss?

Compare all three of your answers.

If you are like most people, your answers to the first question often tend to focus on the material world: buying beach houses, getting that dream sailboat, traveling the world, and so on. Answers to the second question tend to go deeper and are divided between personal accomplishments and family focus: "I'd be a better grandfather," for instance. Answers to the third question typically result in the most profound responses, focus on family and other relationships and thus indicate what's really most important to you—things you would regret not having said or done if your life were cut short.

You have now determined what is most meaningful and significant to you in retirement. These are things that really matter to you. This is not to say that you should neglect finer, more selfish pursuits in life. They can be very enriching on their own and greatly contribute to the quality of your life. But, many years from now, laying on your deathbed, the number of cruises you took to the Caribbean will seem unimportant. How fulfilling and comfortable was your life? Did you achieve a sense of purpose, accomplishment, and balance? What kind of a parent or grandparent were you? What legacy did you leave for your family, church, or educational institution?

Now, if you've done Kinder's exercise with some level of seriousness, look again at the Three Undeniable Goals of Great Investors. Defining your long-term objectives should be a little easier.

The Three Undeniable Goals of all Great Investors

1. Comfortable worry-free income as long as we live.

2. Having ample financial resources to better the lives of children, grandchildren, family members, or others who are important to us.

3. Creating a legacy for family members, charities, or institutions of our choice.

Chapter Summary

♦ Setting your sights on your long-term investment objectives and ignoring short-term distractions can liberate you from sleepless nights.

♦ Investments are tools. That's all. They are a means to an end. Defining the end first makes selecting the means to get there much easier.

*I find television very educating. Every time somebody turns on
the set I go into the other room and read a book.*

—Groucho Marx

15

Great Investors Ignore Short-Term Noise*

Let's get a few things straight right now about the media as a source of trusted financial advice and guidance:

Finance magazines, newspapers, and cable news networks are in the business of selling advertising and attracting viewers.

They are not paid to help people achieve their financial goals.

They get paid to attract eyeballs toward their advertisers—on a daily basis. They have no economic interest in, or knowledge of, your hopes and dreams for retirement.

---

*   Translation: Beware the media and its incessant assault on your common sense.

When you tune in to the news in the evening, you will never hear the newscaster say, "The Dow Jones Industrial Average plummeted 200 points today, but of course, that doesn't really matter if you invest for the long term." No, he simply says, "The Dow Jones plummeted 200 points today." Why? Because, that's news, and that's what makes people watch. The providers of financial news have no particular interest in your personal investing achievements or failures—they are there simply to provide the news of the day in a way that will make you tune in tomorrow. This is largely true of all financial news sources.

Don't Believe Everything You Read

A study was done in which the stock selections of a popular finance magazine* were analyzed from 1/1/90–12/31/94. Here were the results:

Annual Stock Selections

	1990	1991	1992	1993	1994	Average Annual Return
Buy Recommendations	-16.70%	38.30%	-13.10%	-5.80%	3.30%	-0.52%
Sell Recommendations	-23.10%	23.40%	83.60%	12.00%	N/A	18.20%
S&P 500	-3.20%	30.60%	7.70%	10%	1.30%	8.70%

So, if you had done precisely the opposite of what this widely read finance magazine had advised, meaning that you bought when they said to sell and vice versa, you would have achieved an 18.2% average annual return on your investment. That equates to more than twice the return of the S&P 500 over the same time period. Following their advice to the letter would have left you with a negative return for the same time period. Does this strike you as a sound resource for counsel and advice?

There is an old saw that is popular among market pundits. It demonstrates their belief that most investor magazines are printing old news. They say that by the time financial magazines depict either a bull or a bear on their covers,

---

* One you probably have seen in your doctor's waiting room.

the markets are usually about to reverse themselves and proceed in exactly the opposite direction.* While these are just anecdotes, they indicate the level of caution an investor should exercise when presented with market information that is presented as authoritative.

Finally, look at these 1995 headlines from the most widely read daily financial newspaper in the world:

January: *"A Grim First Quarter"*
                (the Dow Jones was up 8% for the first quarter)

March: *"Exercise More Caution"*
                (the Dow was up 9.6% for the second quarter)

July: *"Wall Street Has Jitters, Despite First Half's Surge"*
                (the Dow was up 5% in third quarter)

September: *"Analysts Expect Fourth Quarter Decline"*
                (Dow was up 6.8% for the fourth quarter)

Now, I don't mean to imply here that purveyors of financial information are deliberately trying to cause damage to your retirement portfolio. There is, however, a vast difference between receiving financial *information* and receiving financial *advice*. This is where the breakdown occurs. We need to clearly understand the distinction:

- ◆   **In· for· ma· tion** (i˘n´• f r• ma-´sh n) *n.* something told; facts learned; news or knowledge.

- ◆   **Ad· vice** (a˘d• vis-´) *n.* opinion about how to solve a problem; counsel; guidance.

—Webster's Dictionary

See the difference? Information can come from any source. Advice should come from someone who knows you, knows your personal circumstances, and has the expertise to render it.

---

*   I could not produce any data to support this saying, but it wouldn't surprise me if it were true. Magazine articles are often written many months in advance of their actual publication date.

If you become ill, you may research your symptoms on the Internet or by reading a medical dictionary. You gather information. But, when it comes time to seek treatment, what do you do? You go to your physician, who is trained to give you proper medical advice and knows your personal circumstances. Why then, would you attempt to perform the financial equivalent of brain surgery on yourself by watching the news or reading about the next hot investment in your dentist office waiting room?

Media Information Overload

Another dysfunctional effect generated by the media is information overload. We also refer to this as "The Paralysis of Analysis." You receive so much information every day, and so much of it seems to conflict, that you become paralyzed. For every market expert predicting a prolonged move upward in the market, there is another equally credible analyst telling you that stocks are going to the dogs. It's no wonder you can't make a decision. Wall Street is notorious for producing reams of factual data. And, if you torture the numbers long enough, they will admit to anything.

By promoting a short-term focus, the media disrupts your focus on your long-term objectives. You will notice that, as you watch the nightly news or tune into one of the financial news shows, the newscasters rarely link their commentary to yesterday's events. Or last week's news. The vast majority of news "information" is focused on the here and now. This has a negative effect on most investors, as it draws their attention away from a rational long-term perspective into a short-term focus. We learned earlier that your retirement will likely last many years, meaning you must adopt a long-term view. The fact is: with the exception of unguided investors, day traders, and speculators, virtually everyone's financial goals have little to do with the day-to-day fluctuations of the markets.

One way to avoid all this confusion is to embrace the simple fact that the *truth* and the *news* are two different things. The truth is:

The Three Undeniable Goals of All Great Investors are all that should drive your investment decisions.

Everything else is either news, or worse yet, noise.

Unless your deadline for accomplishing all of your goals is tomorrow, does it really matter what the stock market did for the last twenty minutes? Instead, reclaim those twenty minutes. Spend them on activities that make life enjoyable for you. That's your reward for sticking to your game plan.

Chapter Summary

♦ The media is a good source of information, but a lousy source of advice.

♦ The media has no interest in or knowledge of your personal hopes, dreams, and aspirations.

No law or ordinance is mightier than understanding.

—*Plato*

16

Great Investors Understand and Embrace the 5 Immutable Laws of Investing

There are some very basic laws related to the markets you must accept to become a Great Investor. It's interesting to note that "experienced" investors will sometimes take exception to one or more of the laws. Note that I used the word experienced instead of successful. There are plenty of experienced investors who lost large chunks of their retirement accounts in the 2000–2003 market meltdown. I'd rather be successful than experienced, and following these laws will help you in that pursuit.

Law 1: The future short-term direction of markets is fundamentally unpredictable and unknowable. You cannot time the markets. Period.

If someone had figured it out by now, they would have taken everyone else's money, and they haven't. Since the beginning of time, there has been a buyer and a seller—a winner and a loser. If someone tells you they know with certainty what the markets will do tomorrow, next month, or next year, run for your life. Whatever they are selling, you don't want. The next 10% move in the markets is both unknowable and unimportant if you have prepared yourself for it.

Look at the following depiction of good ("bull") markets and bad ("bear") markets since 1949. You don't need to decipher the chart—just look at the obvious lack of a discernable pattern:

Market Cycles
Bull and Bear Markets 6/13/1949 - 12/31/2005

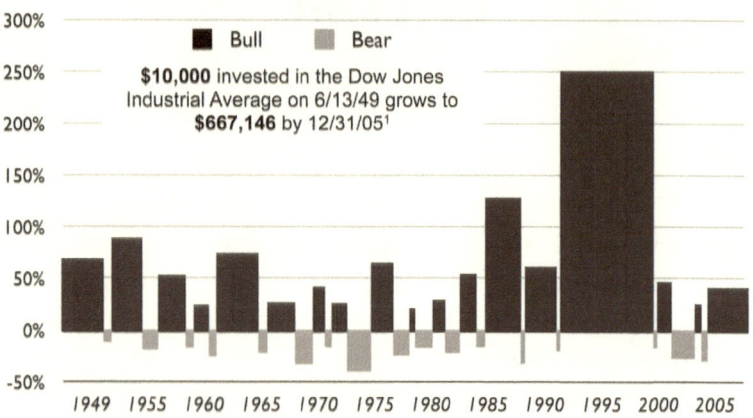

INDEX PAST PERFORMANCE IS NOT INDICATIVE OF FUTURE RESULTS.
Source: Ned Davis Research, 12/05.
[1] Dow Jones Industrial Average (DJIA) is a price -weighted average of 30 actively traded blue-chip stocks, primarily industrials. Dow Jones IndustrialAverage (DJIA) is unmanaged and does not represent the performance of any particular investment. You cannot directly invest in the DJIA.

The notion that someone has the clairvoyance to predict with any level of accuracy tomorrow's bull or bear market is nonsense. Further, the notion they would share it with you for the cost of a newsletter is simply nuts. From this, we can draw the following conclusion: We will probably continue to have both bull and bear markets in your remaining lifetime, and attempting to predict them in advance is not a good use of your time. The fallacy of market timing is best illustrated with an example:

> *Meet Larry, Moe, Curly, and Shemp. Beginning on 12/31/79, each is given $2,000 a year to invest. Larry times the market perfectly every single year and puts his money in the stocks of the S&P 500 at the end of the month that has the lowest closing price of the year. Moe, being lazy, puts his money in the S&P 500 each year-end and leaves it there. Curly, the worst market timer ever, invests in the S&P 500 at the end of the month that has the highest price of the year—every year. Shemp, who's afraid of the stock market, buys Treasury bills.*

Results after 20 years:

- Larry, the perfect market timer:

    $387,120
- Moe, the buy-and-hold investor:

    $362,185
- Curly, the poor market timer:

    $321,569
- Shemp, the T-bill investor:

    $76,558

What's surprising is that Larry, with perfect market timing sense (which we know doesn't exist), does only a little better than Moe, who adheres to the buy-and-hold philosophy. On the other hand, poor Curly tries to time the markets and does horribly, 11% less than Moe. And Shemp, who purchased T-bills because they are "safe", wasn't even in the running.[42]

Here's another good example to help you understand the folly of market timing:

Over the 10 years ended Dec. 31, 2001, the S&P returned an annual average of more than 12%. There were approximately 2,500 trading days in this time period. What happens if you miss a few good days because you are sitting on the sidelines?[43]

The Folly of Market Timing

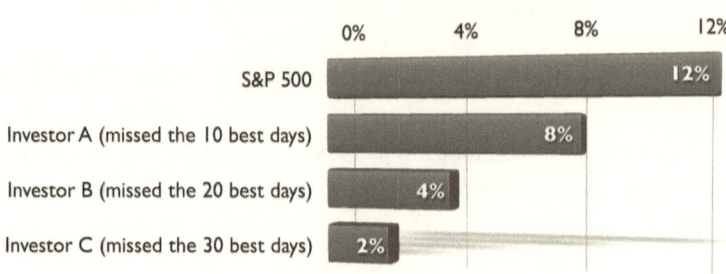

Over the 10 years ended Dec. 31, 2001, the S&P returned an annual average of
more than 12%. There were approximately 2,500 trading days in this time period.

Franklin Templeton Investments, 2006

The conclusion: market timing is a fool's errand.

Law 2: Diversification and time leach almost all of the risk out of a portfolio of quality investments.

Take a wooden match. It's fairly easy to break, correct? Now, bind ten wooden matches together with a rubber band and try it. Not so easy, is it? The risk of only owning a few individual investments is too excessive. Remember, diversification means spreading your assets across many investments—like binding the matches together.

> *Let's say Fred and Barney each have $10,000 to invest. Fred uses the entire amount to purchase U.S. government bonds paying 5.25%.*
> *Barney, however, decides to spread his nest egg among five different types of investments. Here are his investment choices and results:*

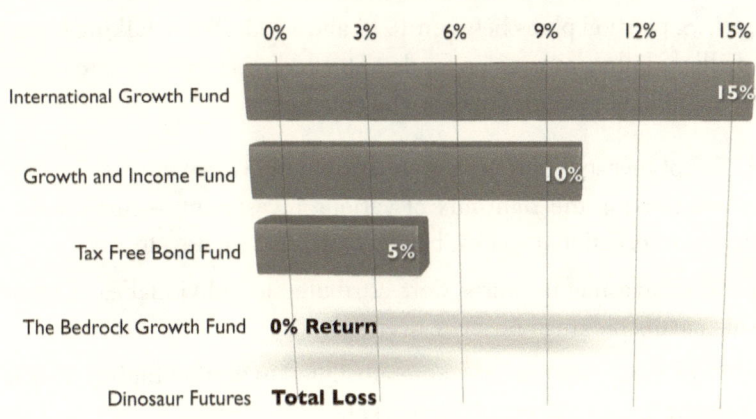

Barney's Investment Choices
$2,000 in Each

You will note that three of Barney's investments do okay, but one only breaks even and the other is a total loss. How badly do these two investments hurt his return? At the end of 25 years, Fred has $54,000 from his $10,000 bond investment. Barney, however, has more than $96,000, roughly 44 percent more than Fred. Diversification, as you're hopefully learning, is a wonderful tool for reducing risk and increasing your long-term returns. It makes even the worst investor look like a pro over the long term.

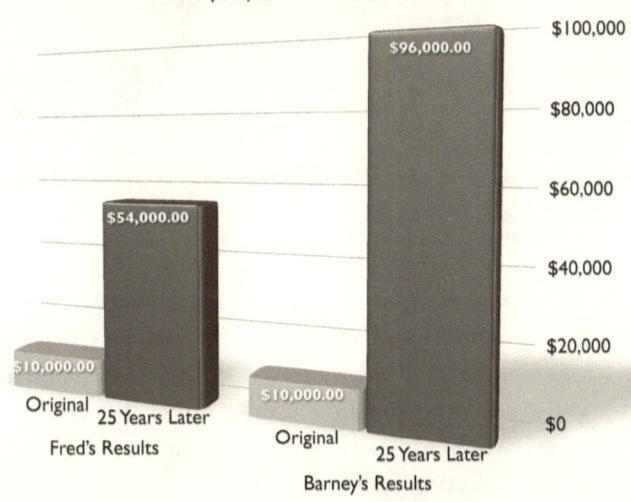

Fred and Barney's Results
$10,000 in Each

There is a mountain of academic support on the subject of diversification as a risk reducer and return enhancer. A 1991 study reviewed the performance of 91 large U.S. pension plans between 1974 and 1983. (We're talking about more than a trillion dollars in pension funds.) The findings are considered a seminal work in the field of modern finance. The conclusions?

◆ 91.5% of investment returns were attributed to asset class selection. That means picking the right mix of various investments—small stocks, big stocks, international stocks, bonds, cash, real estate, etc.

◆ 4.1% of investment returns were attributed to individual stock selection. This means picking one stock over another.

◆ 1.7% of investment returns were attributed to market timing. This means choosing to be in or out of the market.

Determinants of Investment Portfolio Profitability

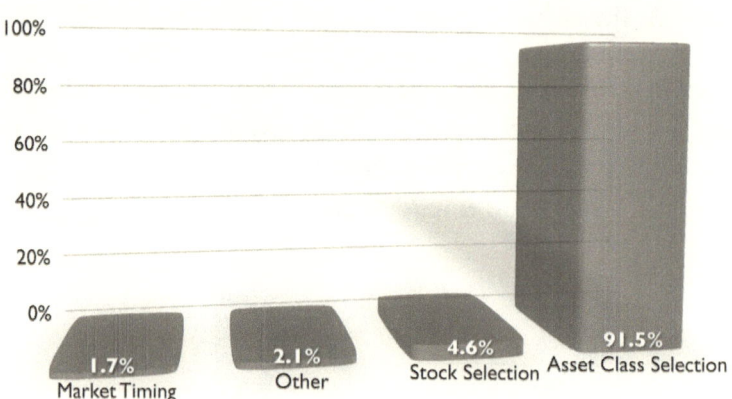

Source: Brinson, Singer and Beebower, "Explanation of Total Return Variation," Financial Analysts Journal, May/June 1991.

So, we learn that more than 90% of available investment returns can be collected by proper diversification of your money to various categories, less than 5% comes from stock picks at the water cooler, and less than 2% comes from your uncanny instinct to be completely in or out of the market. Hello? Anyone home? Why on earth would you spend a single moment of your time or money on anything other than door number one?

If you're still a little confused about diversification, here's an easy way to understand it. Ever been across the Golden Gate Bridge in San Francisco? You have wonderfully panoramic views of the Bay. The Bridge has six lanes. Do you recall which lane you used to drive across the bay? Probably not. Let's assume the bridge had no guardrails to protect you from plummeting into the bay. Which lane would you use? Correct—the middle one.

Well, since no one knows which assets (stocks, bonds, etc.) will do well and which will do poorly next year, owning a mix of them can provide you with a smoother ride across the middle lane of investing. By spreading your investment dollars across a variety of investments with different risk characteristics, you minimize the effect of one specific type of risk on your portfolio, thereby avoiding driving off the bridge in our example. "But," you protest, "When one of my investments does well, I will only reap part of the benefit instead of the whole thing." True enough. Diversification ensures that you won't make a killing in one specific investment. It also ensures that you won't get killed when that investment does poorly. Remember—no one knows what tomorrow's winner will be, and chasing yesterday's winner is a losing game. Diversification keeps you focused on the middle lane.

Next to diversification, time is the most important consideration for minimizing risk. History tells us that if you purchased a diversified portfolio of quality stocks today and sold it tomorrow, you stand about a 70% chance of making versus losing money. But, look what happens to your chances of making money over different time periods.[44]

Average Historical Returns on Stocks for Various Holding Periods: 1925-2003

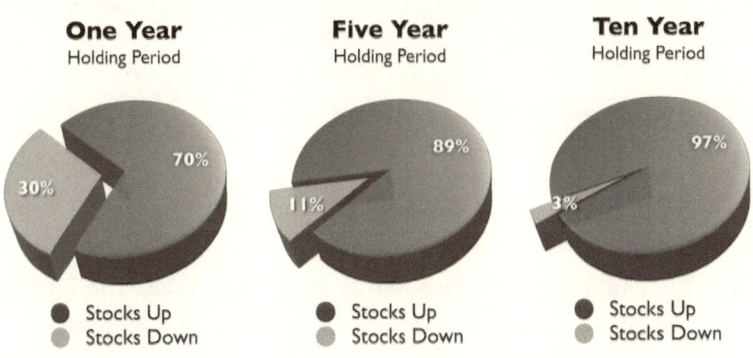

Returns on S&P 500 12/31/1925-12/31/2003. Assumes reinvestment of dividends and no transaction costs. Source: Weisenberger, 1/04

Owning stocks for short periods of time is certainly riskier than owning fixed income investments. But, as you will see shortly, stocks (as a group) have soundly thumped all other asset classes over longer periods of time. So, time and diversification are our most powerful tools for minimizing risk and maximizing return.

Law 3: The stock and bond markets have periodically gone down, but they haven't stayed down.

Let me be clear. I didn't say, "All investments go down, but don't stay down." Plenty of them have gone down to zero and stayed there. The markets in general, however, have been going up since their inception with periodic fluctuations in value. It's true, the overall markets can and do decline. But they also advance. And, over time, they have advanced splendidly.

Let's look at the following chart. I don't want you to interpret it. Just look at where all the lines start, where they end, and the pattern they follow to get there.

Investment Comparisons

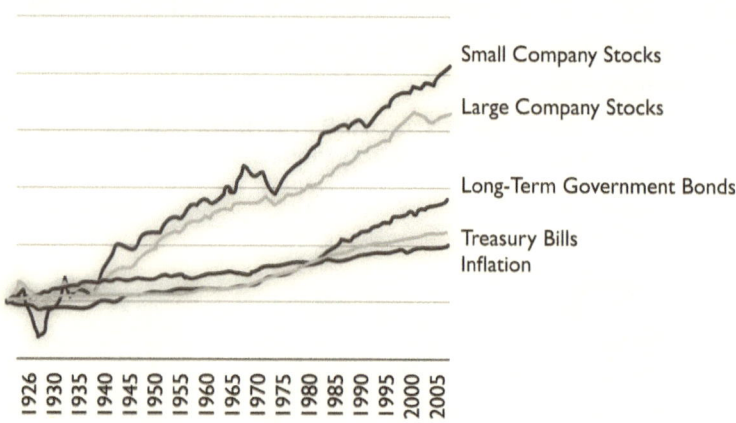

I offer this chart not to confuse, but to clarify my point. The investments with the smoothest lines (the least market risk) have gone up over time. But, the investments with the more jagged lines (more fluctuation in value) have gone up significantly more.

Here's the law within a law. This is a fundamental truth, and you need to accept it:

The price we pay for market advances is market declines. If the declines went away, then the advances would go away too.

You get rewarded for the risk of declines with the prospect of advances.

Fear of market declines is generally driven by a short-term focus. We can thank the media for this, who I roundly chastised earlier. This fear is easily banished by a little perspective.

Nick Murray, a highly respected author and financial industry veteran, coined this advance/decline rule and is a master at providing the proper perspective. I recall hearing him once say, "Isn't it wonderful to live in a country where the stock market has been going up your entire life?" He went on to explain that, while it certainly hasn't gone straight up, the markets have been advancing since you were born, regardless of your age. How's that for perspective? In the past century, we've witnessed wars, political crises, recessions, the Great Depression, terrorism on our soil, and a host of other economic, cultural and political challenges. In spite of all this, the markets and our economy have—over the long term—continued their march upward and rewarded patience with increased wealth. Market declines represent nothing more than a buying opportunity for Great Investors. As unguided investors[*] are running for the exits, Great Investors calmly walk the aisles in the financial supermarket, looking for bargains. "Oh, look! Investments are on sale today. Think I'll buy some."

If you have another two or three decades to live, I would suggest that maintaining the proper perspective will reward you handsomely, and fretting about next week's earnings reports will not.

---

[*] A.k.a. "dumb money"

Law 4: Stocks have historically done better over time than bonds.

As we have discussed previously, conventional wisdom held that when you retired, you should shift all your investment and retirement assets into fixed annuities, bonds, and bank instruments like CDs. This may have been a perfectly acceptable strategy when your average life expectancy at retirement was less than a decade, but it can be devastating if you plan to be around a while. Here's why:

When you purchase bonds or CDs, you are loaning a company (or the government or a bank) your money. The company promises to give you two things in return:

◆   A fixed amount of interest on the loan you've made to them—no more and no less.

◆   Your original money back at some future point—no more and no less.

Let's say you loan the government $10.00. In exchange, they agree to pay you 5%, or 50¢ per year, for twenty years, and then give you your $10.00 back. You are delighted, because your living expenses are only 30¢ per year.

Each year, you happily collect your 50¢. After you give Uncle Sam his 28% (bond income is taxable at ordinary income rates), you'll have 38¢ to live on—a comfortable margin, since you only require 30¢. We'll assume inflation runs at 3%.

In year ten, your living expenses have risen to 39¢ due to inflation. But, you protest, I'm only keeping 38¢ after taxes. I need more income! What will you do? You're only halfway through your deal with the government. If inflation continues at the assumed rate, things will only get worse. Unfortunately, your options are limited. You can either sell your bond and live off the ten dollars in the hope that you expire before it does, or make painful choices and adjust your lifestyle for your lower fixed income level.

It is a fact that stocks can and do fluctuate in value. It is also a fact that, over time, they have historically delivered higher returns—in the form of future income—to investors. Let's look at another example. Assume it's 1977 and you are retiring with $100,000. Let's assume a 30 year time horizon. You need retirement income. You are presented with three options for investing your $100,000:

Your first option is to invest in a CD, which will have varying levels of income year-to-year. Let's assume you do. Here's what your annual income and principal value would look like through the beginning of 2007:

Income from CDs

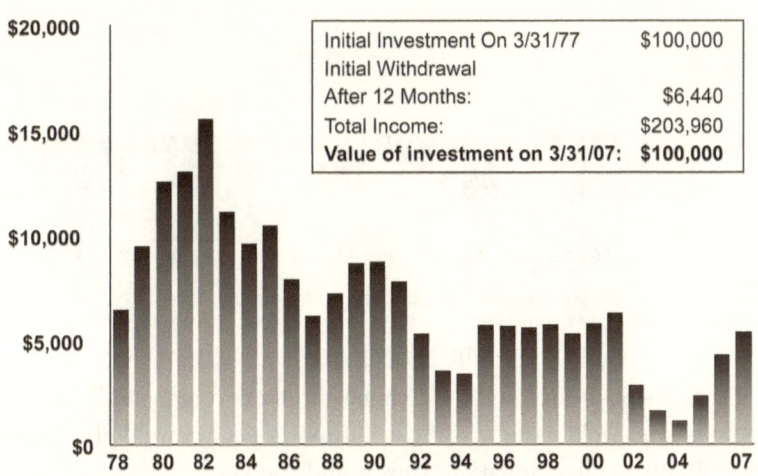

Initial Investment On 3/31/77	$100,000
Initial Withdrawal After 12 Months:	$6,440
Total Income:	$203,960
Value of investment on 3/31/07:	**$100,000**

Data Source: Lipper Inc. 4/07

So, you started with $100,000 and ended with $100,000 thirty years later. Your income stream fluctuated with CD rates, and the last few years haven't been all that attractive.

Your second option is to purchase a 30-year treasury bond, which is yielding a handsome 5% annual coupon rate. Each year, you can count on $5,000 in income from your bond.

After 30 years, you would have received a total of $150,000 in income. Then, you would get your original $100,000 back.

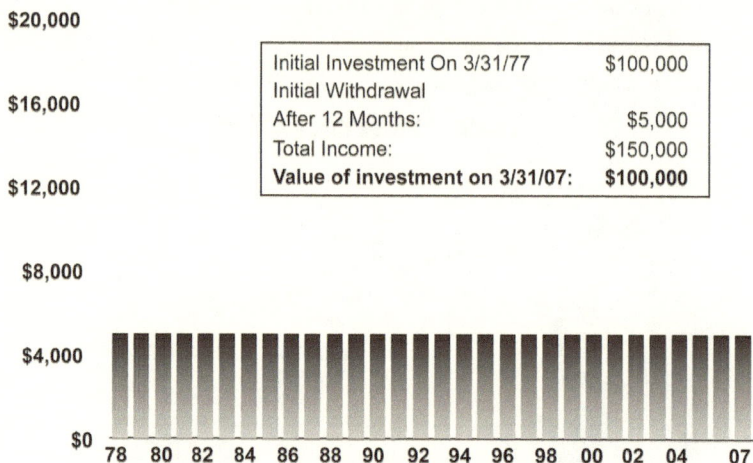

Income from Government Bonds*
Flat Income

Initial Investment On 3/31/77	$100,000
Initial Withdrawal	
After 12 Months:	$5,000
Total Income:	$150,000
Value of investment on 3/31/07:	**$100,000**

*Based on a 5% coupon.

Option 3 is to build a portfolio of 60% stocks and 40% bonds. Let's use the S&P 500 as a stock proxy and the Lehman Brothers Aggregate Bond Index to represent bonds. We'll assume a 5% withdrawal rate, but we'll also increase it by 4% annually to offset inflation. How would you fare?

Income from Portfolio of 60% Stocks/40% Bonds

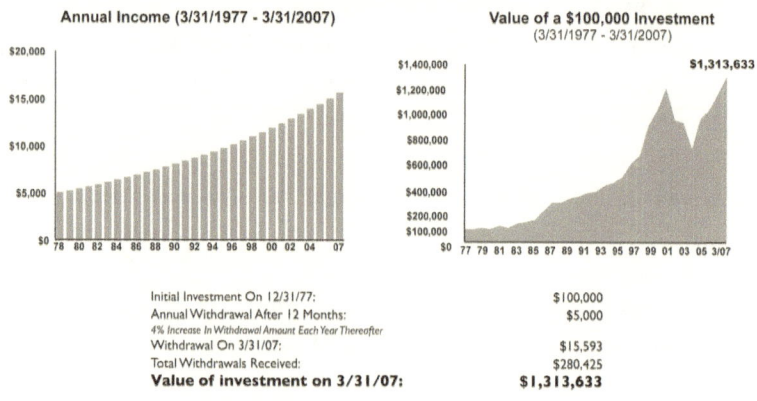

Annual Income (3/31/1977 - 3/31/2007)

Value of a $100,000 Investment
(3/31/1977 - 3/31/2007)

$1,313,633

Initial Investment On 12/31/77:	$100,000
Annual Withdrawal After 12 Months:	$5,000
4% Increase In Withdrawal Amount Each Year Thereafter	
Withdrawal On 3/31/07:	$15,593
Total Withdrawals Received:	$280,425
Value of investment on 3/31/07:	**$1,313,633**

Equity investments are generally more volatile than other types of investments.

These examples are for illustrative purposes only. Charts assume reinvestment of dividends and capital gains. Taxes and transaction costs were not taken into account. Note that performance would have been lower if taxes were taken into account. Data Source: Thompson Financial Software, 4/07.

So with a total of 60% stocks and 40% bonds, you received total income of $280,000 for the 30 year period (significantly more than options #1 and #2), and your ending account value thirty years later was in excess of $1.3 million.

Once again, it is important to recognize that the conventional wisdom of simply owning fixed income investments can seriously jeopardize your potential to create greater wealth and an increasing income stream to offset inflation. Equity-based portfolios have, over time, been wonderfully efficient at producing a growing income stream.

Now, before you run out and reallocate all your retirement assets, read and review Law #5 closely.

Law 5. Past performance is no guarantee of the future, but it's all we've got.

The business of providing investment advice and financial planning counsel is a highly regulated one. The self-regulatory organizations have done a fine job of ensuring the average consumer is exposed to all the risks, charges, and expenses of any particular investment opportunity, and that unscrupulous insurance agents or financial advisors are restricted from projecting unrealistic returns to dress up a sales pitch. (This is also known as "perfuming the pig.") Virtually every illustration, prospectus, or sales brochure will be prominently labeled with the following warning:

Past performance is no guarantee of future results.

The simple fact is that we do not know how a particular investment allocation will do tomorrow, next week, or next year. But, we do know how those investment allocations have done in the past through both good and bad markets, because we have a record of their performance. This is instructive, as we can now run any series of imaginable future economic situations and project how a group of assets might perform together to give us greater predictability of our potential future outcome. This is investment science at its best. Note that history will most assuredly not repeat itself exactly, and your result may in fact vary to a material degree, but it remains the best option we have for constructing a realistic plan.

In addition, we have been both blessed and cursed over the past decade or so. We have seen an extraordinary bull market, followed by a devastating bear market, followed by a four-year market recovery. This allows us to look at how certain assets performed through this cycle, and how certain assets performed when owned alongside other assets during this time period. There are no crystal balls. No one knows what tomorrow may bring, and past performance may not be a predictor of the future, but it sure beats a Ouija Board or a Magic 8 Ball.

Chapter Summary

♦ The Five Immutable Laws of Investing are nothing more than a combination of history, perspective, and common sense.

♦ There's no guarantee that history will repeat itself, but it's pretty much all we have to rely upon to draw conclusions about the future.

Section IV

In strategy it is important to see distant things as if they were close and to take a distanced view of close things.

—*Miyamoto Musashi*

17

Developing a RICHER™ Retirement Strategy

Now that we have acquired the basic financial literacy required to make sound investment decisions, let's use them in a strategy I developed called the RICHER™ Retirement Strategy. This strategy is designed specifically to immunize you against the Five Key Risks we have identified that could disrupt your retirement. The name is no accident. Who among us wouldn't want a richer retirement strategy? "But", you exclaim, "I already have a plan for retirement. I have my 401(k) at work; I have two IRA's, some savings, and a brokerage account. Therefore, I am set."

With all due respect, that's not a plan—it's a list. You need to develop a strategy which addresses every aspect of your financial life in retirement and ensures all your financial assets are tied to a specific objective.

First, let's establish an estimate of your required retirement income. There is no scientific formula that will render a correct answer here, as each individual's circumstances, lifestyle, and post-retirement income need is different. Generally, most experts estimate your required retirement income should be between 70% and 85% of your pre-retirement income. (I have seen many cases where retirees are perfectly happy with 50% of their pre-retirement income, and others where more than 100% was required. Again, it's based on your personal circumstance and lifestyle needs.) In his book, *The Number*, Lee Eisenberg offers some general guidelines for how much post retirement income you will require based on your lifestyle:

How Much Will You Need?

To be...	you need...	which means a number of...
Comfortable: lives in one home, eats, & travels modestly, though better than most	$50K - $100K	$1-2 million
Comfortable+: likes occasional upgrade, mid-priced country club, a small second home	$175K - $250K	$2-5 million
Kind of Rich: likes finer things, eats/drinks/travels well, gives money away, picks up checks, couple of nice houses	$350K-$500K	$7-10 million
Rich: spends weeks/months abroad, exclusive gated golf communities, place for every season, fractional jets, sits on boards	> $1 million	> $20 million

Source: Lee Eisenberg, "The Number" January 2006

So, if your pre-retirement income is $100,000, you should generally shoot for $70,000 to $85,000 of post-retirement income from all sources for a comfortable lifestyle.* We will use the benchmark of $100,000 of pre-retirement income and a goal of $75,000 of post retirement income throughout this illustration.

In my RICHER™ Retirement Strategy, each letter represents a particular element of a comprehensive retirement strategy. Let's explore the strategy together.

---

* And, we'll need to make sure that income stream grows to offset inflation.

18

R: Reserve Strategy

Any decent retirement plan ensures you have adequate reserves for life's unanticipated turns. Autos break down, homes need repairing, driveways need resurfacing, and irresponsible grandchildren need money to have tattoos removed. The objective of your reserve strategy is to provide the necessary resources to weather short term storms without disrupting your long-term cash flows or compromising those precious assets you might need down the road. Note that reserves are not a source of monthly income. This is your "dry powder" for tomorrow's unexpected emergency. You want to wring every penny of returns available out of these assets, since you do not anticipate needing them anytime soon.

I generally break your reserves into two categories—short-term reserves, which are typically three months of average living expenses—and long-term reserves—typically another nine months of living expenses. Why do you need 12 months of living expenses in reserves? Recall that your longer-term assets can and should fluctuate in value over time. (Remember the Five Immutable Laws?) Without reserves, you may be forced to tap into your long-term assets at a time when the markets are experiencing a downturn, depleting your long-term assets by a larger percentage. If you have created a diversified long-term portfolio, you must give it an opportunity to work for you. Thus, we have our Reserve accounts.

If your annual post-retirement income need is $75,000 per our earlier assumption, then you will need approximately $18,750 in short term reserves. ($75,000 divided by 12 months = $6,250 x 3 months = $18,750.)

I generally recommend that the short-term reserves are placed in one of the following, depending upon market conditions and personal circumstances:

♦ Tax-free money market accounts

♦ Taxable money market accounts

♦ CDs or other liquid investments

♦ High yield savings accounts

As I mentioned earlier, bank CDs are perfectly fine investments for short-term assets. But, you need to ensure you are earning the highest rate possible. It is a common misconception that bank CD and money market rates are purely a function of national interest rate levels, and they are all basically the same. While national interest rates certainly set the bar, banks will either raise or lower the rate they are willing to offer investors based on that banks need for fresh capital. Banks are simply borrowing money from you, paying you a stated rate of interest, and loaning your money to others at a higher interest rate. This is a perfectly acceptable arrangement. The rate they are willing to pay you is a function of their need for new capital. It has been my experience that you can often find more attractive rates from local banks rather than large national banks, as local bank needs for capital are more dependent on the local economy. National banks have branches all over the country collecting deposits, and therefore may be less willing to raise local rates to attract deposits. Local banks also offer a more personal relationship opportunity, which is important to us all.

Your long-term reserve is equal to nine months of your annual requirement, or $56,250. It should be invested in a diversified, conservative investment portfolio focused on wealth preservation. You may also wish to use longer term CDs for this portion if interest rates are acceptably higher than short term rates.

We wish to have the opportunity for this money to grow since we don't anticipate needing it, but we require liquidity for reasons already mentioned. There are many excellent mutual funds out there that offer capital preservation as an investment objective. By taking a bit of principal risk, we receive the potential for a higher rate of return than we might see on principal guaranteed investments such as short term CDs. Review the track record of any potential long-term reserve options to see how it has performed in both good and bad economic times. Again, while your principal may fluctuate a bit, that's the tradeoff for higher potential returns over time on money we don't expect to need.

Any time you draw upon your short or long-term reserves, you should immediately begin replenishing the withdrawal from your monthly retirement cash flows, if possible, to replace the funds you have taken. This allows your longer-term assets to continue to work for you uninterrupted.

Chapter Summary

♦ Maintaining adequate reserves allows your longer-term investments to do what they are designed to do—produce potentially higher income for you in the future.

♦ Having a years worth of living expenses at your fingertips gives you a sense of control and liquidity to help you sleep better at night.

19

I: Insured Income Strategy

First, let's articulate what we mean here by "insured income."

In my view, insured income means that your check will arrive regardless of rain, sleet, snow, stock market performance, the economy, geopolitical turmoil, and other unknowable future events. Insured income is wonderfully predictable and stable, in that it is impervious to all these external forces. The ability to maintain your lifestyle without regard to the daily machinations of the markets is a desirable outcome, I'm sure you would agree. Well, there are only three sources of insured income available to you—pensions, Social Security, and annuities. That's it. Let's look a little closer at each one.

If you have a pension provided by a private company or civil service employer, you should be able to depend upon that pension in retirement to produce insured income. These guarantees are based upon the financial solvency of the company or civil service employer providing them. I have conducted countless retirement education workshops for employers who offer pensions, and I continue to be astounded by the number of employees who see their pension as having little value as an employee benefit. A couple of points are worth noting here.

First, pension assets typically consist of a contribution by the employer and the employee each pay period. When you retire, the employer guarantees you a stable source of income no matter how long you live or no matter how well your pension assets perform. So, let's make a deal. Say you retire at 60. I'll give you all the money you and your employer contributed into the pension plan during your working life. You are on your own. Are you comfortable that you could make that asset last as long as you (and your spouse) live? What if you make poor choices with investments? Who pays the cost of those mistakes? You do. With a pension, however, the risk is entirely on the employer and they pay the cost of poor market performance. Your checks still arrive every two weeks.

Second, we learned earlier that everyone is living longer. Assume you worked for twenty five years and retired at age 55 with a pension. Further, let's assume that your spouse is 50. If you live to be 85, and your spouse lives to be 90, it is entirely possible that you and your spouse will receive total pension benefits *in excess of your earned wages during your entire career*. I would suggest this represents a pretty good deal. Based on my research, pension benefits will be the most coveted of assets in the next few decades. If you have one, you should start paying closer attention to it and ensure your employer realizes its value to employees.

Social Security, which we addressed in morbid detail earlier in this book, is based upon the ability of the Federal Government and your representatives in Washington to foot the bill for your benefits through taxation.*

Finally, annuities are investments provided by insurance companies and are designed to provide certain guarantees with regard to safety of your principal and promises of stable income. In my view, they will play an invaluable role in the future filling in the gap for the decline in pensions and potential Social Security shortfalls. Despite what opinions you may hold of insurance companies or annuities, I suspect they will become the most viable provider of insurable income for many Americans approaching retirement.

Now, before I am accused of shilling for insurance companies, let me state that I have no love for these companies in particular. But I must confess that in the last few years, they have realized that a sizeable portion of our population will have limited sources of insured income in retirement. As a result, annuity providers have created a new generation of benefits which offer very compelling features emphasizing the three things retired investors need from an insured income source: control, liquidity, and security.

---

*   As we have explored earlier, one should proceed with caution when making assumptions about Social Security benefits and the taxation of those benefits. Only time will tell.

In order to provide an objective and independent understanding of annuities, you must first suspend any preconceived notions you may have about them. When I set out to write this book, I decided I would not spend any time at all apologizing for the past sins of unscrupulous insurance agents and self-interested brokers of the past. Let's lay down a universal truth in the world of investment advice:

There's no such thing as a good or bad investment. It's the circumstances under which an investment is purchased that make it good or bad.

In my experience, general knowledge regarding annuities falls into one of three categories:

♦ Annuities are carcinogens. I don't know why, and I don't care, but I've never heard a kind word said about them, so they must be bad for me.

♦ I once bought an annuity, and I'm not really sure why or what it's supposed to do for me.

♦ What's an annuity?

Here's a very brief primer on traditional annuities. In 1653, a Neapolitan banker named Lorenzo Tonti developed a method for raising money in France called the tontine. Under this arrangement, subscribers purchased shares in exchange for income generated from the capital investment. As shareholders died off, their income was spread among the surviving partners until the last person alive collected all the benefits. The use of tontines spread to Britain and the United States where governments used them to finance public works projects. The tontine was an early predecessor to today's annuity.

An annuity is nothing more than a contract between you and an insurance company. That's it. You give them a sum of money, and they make certain guarantees to you regarding your money.* It's equally important to note that

---

* It's important to understand that those guarantees are backed by the ability of the company to meet their obligations and not by the government, which we'll discuss later.

when you give your money to any other investment provider where there is market risk, there are no guarantees. Period. Remember this well.

It is an indisputable fact that annuities have sometimes been sold to unknowing people by unscrupulous insurance agents and advisors interested in making a commission. (This practice has not been limited to annuities and is true with virtually every investment under the sun, but I digress.) It is remarkable how much hullabaloo has been generated about annuities considering that less than 5% of American households currently own one. They have been maligned by self-professed personal finance mavens, waiting room periodicals, and others who claim to have your personal best interests at heart. The media, which we have already properly identified as having no personal interest in your financial security and success, have fanned the flames of discontent based upon their incessant desire to sell more newspapers and magazines. Remember, that's their business. It's not uncommon to see the press refer to annuities and investment scams in the same sentence. It's all nonsense, in my view. You simply cannot tar any investment with a "good" or "bad" brush. You must examine the circumstance under which that investment is being considered. If you have limited pension and/or Social Security income in retirement, annuities may be your best option for insuring additional stable retirement income.

From a mechanical perspective, annuities have traditionally had a few universal features:

Tax Deferral

Your contributions to an annuity grow tax deferred, meaning you pay no tax on it until you begin withdrawing funds. Once you begin withdrawing money, you pay ordinary income taxes only on the amount you withdraw. Further, you only pay income tax on the earnings. Any return of principal to you is not taxed.

Death Benefit

Should you die when you own an annuity, your beneficiaries will receive either the amount you put in less withdrawals, or its current value, whichever is higher. For example, assume you purchase an annuity for $100,000. Let's say the market plummets, and upon receiving your first statement, you notice your value has dropped to $75,000. The shock gives you a heart attack, and you die. Your beneficiaries would receive $100,000.

Fixed or Variable Investment Options

Annuities offer the option of investing in fixed return instruments (such as bonds), or variable return instruments such as mutual funds and stocks.

Guaranteed Lifetime Income

In the past, if you decided that you wanted guaranteed predictable income you couldn't outlive, you effectively surrendered your cash value back to the insurance company, and they ensured you received a fixed income stream you could not outlive. This is referred to as "annuitization" and still exists as an option on virtually all annuities. There are, in my view, some fundamental drawbacks to annuitization as a strategy for guaranteed lifetime income.

First, annuitization requires you to give up the asset itself. It's no longer yours, and you cannot change your mind about it later. You have essentially traded the asset for a guarantee of future fixed income. Second, you are typically trading the asset for a fixed annual income amount—no more and no less. As we have learned, a growing stream of income will be required to offset inflation in the future, and typical fixed annuities generally do not accommodate for this.

In the recent past, variable annuity companies have realized that these basic features weren't particularly appealing to a generation that expects to live another 30 or 40 years and needs a rising income stream to ward off inflation. They also realized that requiring individuals to give up control of the asset for a guaranteed lifetime income was not going to fly for future retirees. So, they have added features commonly referred to as "living benefits". These benefits have some very appealing properties, such as:

♦   A guarantee that the least I (or my heirs) will receive back from my annuity investment is the amount I put in less any withdrawals I take. In effect, my principal is guaranteed in the form of retirement income for me and my family.

♦ A guarantee that if my annuity investment (typically in mutual funds and other diversified investments) rises in value, the amount of income I can receive from it will rise accordingly and not go down for the rest of my life (and that of my spouse, if I choose). And I still retain the right to the principal value of the asset if I'm unhappy and wish to take it elsewhere.

♦ A guarantee that, if I delay taking income today, the amount of income I can receive in the future will rise annually until such time as I begin taking income, regardless of market performance.

♦ A guarantee that I can request my capital back at any time if I'm unsatisfied with my performance.*

Sound too good to be true? Well, it isn't. But as with all investments, you need to understand all the risks and costs well enough to make an informed decision. There are four key areas you need to fully investigate and understand regarding annuities. They are designed to be long-term investments. The aforementioned guarantees are based on an assumption that you plan on sticking around long enough to benefit from them. They also tend to have a lot of moving parts, and it's important to understand the benefits, expenses, and risks. I strongly suggest you consult an independent financial advisor to help you understand them. The key areas to understand are:

Credit Quality of the Annuity Company

The guarantees in your annuity are only as good as the company issuing them. There are more than 500 insurance companies in this country. When you screen out those companies that maintain an A+ rating or higher[45], there are approximately 16. If someone is going to make these contractual agreements with you and your family, I would suggest you want to ensure they will be around for the next century to honor their obligations. This means sticking with the companies that have been around through thick and thin for the past 100 or so years.

---

* Note: Some annuities contain surrender charges, which I'll cover shortly.

Fees and Expenses

Every annuity carries a basic Mortality and Expense ("M&E") charge. These are the base charges incurred by an annuity company to set up and administer the annuity, insure the death benefits, and pay an advisor for recommending it to you. You'll want to investigate these fees, as they can vary widely depending upon a number of factors.

Next, there are rider fees. The living benefits I listed above typically come packaged as a "rider", an option similar to the ones you can purchase with a new car. Rider fees can vary depending upon the features and the expenses of the annuity company to ensure it can meet its obligations to you.

Finally, there are the internal fees associated with the underlying investments, which are typically mutual funds. All these fees are typically deducted from the gross investment returns on your annuity before you are credited with your net returns. For example, assume the total fees and expenses on your annuity are 2.5%. Let's assume your underlying investments have a total gross return for the year of 12.5%. Your net return after fees and expenses would be 10%.

Now, one of the favorite points of the media is that variable annuities are too expensive. To which I respond, "Compared to what?" What other investment alternative offers the four benefits mentioned just a moment ago? In order to answer the question of expense, you would have to rationally address the question this way: Can I achieve a similar financial and economic outcome for myself for lower cost another way?" If the answer is no, then it's not too expensive.

You will, however, want to keep your total fees and expenses for an annuity as low as possible, as every dime of expense is a dime out of your returns and your future income stream. Make sure you do some comparisons of total fees prior to selecting an annuity.

Surrender Charges

All of your money goes to work for you immediately in an annuity. There is no front-end commission charge taken from your initial investment. But, annuity companies do incur expenses for establishing your annuity. They have to pay the advisor for recommending the annuity to you, and they incur various administrative costs for establishing an annuity contract. They protect themselves by imposing a surrender charge if you should surrender your annuity in the early years after establishing the annuity contract. If you decide to withdraw all your money within a few years of establishing it, the company would sustain a loss based on its initial costs and expenses. Variable annuities typically offer surrender periods that range from zero years to ten years, depending upon the company, contract features, and internal expenses. The charge usually declines over the period of time you own the annuity.

Penalties for Early Withdrawal

Since annuities accumulate on a tax-deferred basis, there could be tax penalties if you take withdrawals prior to age 59 ½. You will need to consult with a tax advisor or your financial advisor for more details here, but remember that you should not purchase an annuity as anything other than a long-term savings and retirement income vehicle.

You should weigh each of these four components carefully and make sure you understand all of them well prior to purchasing an annuity. Again, an advisor can help you sort through all the fine print to make sure you fully understand the charges, expenses, and risks before selecting an annuity.

So, how might one of these annuities create more insured income for you in retirement?

Let's stick with our previous example. Say you are planning to retire at age 60, and you've calculated you'll need $75,000 of annual income in retirement. Your insured income from your pension and Social Security totals $37,500, or 50% of your required retirement income. This means you'll need to get $37,500 per year from your investment assets. That may be easy in some years, and more difficult in others, depending upon the size of your portfolio, your asset allocation, and how well the markets cooperate.

Assume you want less market risk, so you place $300,000 into an annuity that offers the following benefits:

♦ A guarantee that you will receive a minimum of 5%, or $15,000 per year as long as you (and your spouse, if you choose) may live, regardless of how well the underlying investments perform.

♦ A guarantee if the underlying investments you choose should rise in value; you may elect to periodically "step-up" your annual income benefit to a higher fixed number for the rest of your life, *regardless of what happens to the underlying actual value in subsequent years.* This can create a rising income stream in good markets, and guarantee a stable income stream in bad markets.

♦ The option to request a return of some or all of your capital based on its current value less any surrender charges due.

This strategy would effectively create a private pension plan for you which, combined with your other sources of insured income, would increase your insured income total from 50% to 70% of your anticipated income need in retirement, with the opportunity for your insured income to rise if the underlying investments perform well.

Here's another way to think about insured income: Generally, successful people don't take much risk. Where possible, they lay the risks off on someone else who is willing to accept it. So, if you can transfer some of the risk of a compromised retirement income stream onto someone else, it may make sense to do so.

Based on all the irrefutable data I provided in the first few chapters of this book, I believe it is vital to make sure you have adequate sources of insured income in retirement. So how much of your total income should be insured versus uninsured? It depends upon your personal circumstances. If you need $75,000 of annual retirement income, how much would you like to come from insured sources versus sources that are susceptible to market fluctuations? At the risk of sounding like a broken record, you may need to engage a qualified financial advisor to help you decide.

Certainly, some level of insured income in retirement is both prudent and comforting.

Chapter Summary

♦ Some level of insured income in retirement is both prudent and comforting.

♦ Recent innovations in the annuity industry allow you to effectively create a synthetic pension plan for yourself to supplement your current pensions and/or Social Security if needed.

20

C: Capital Growth and Income Strategy

Now that we have allocated a comfortable reserve, and we have calculated and solved for our insured income need, we must ensure our remaining retirement assets are allocated for both capital growth and income for reasons I hope are obvious to you by now. We need to grow our assets, so our income can grow to offset the effects of inflation. If we are using our capital growth assets to supplement our insured income, then we need to construct a portfolio that can provide us with a long-term rate of return in excess of our withdrawal rate so our income can grow accordingly. How do we pick such a portfolio? Let's refer back to history here to help us determine a particular asset allocation that might suit us. Take a look at the following historical returns from 1926–2006. Pay particular attention to the best one-year, worst one-year, and average annual performance for each portfolio. Now, ask yourself, "Which one of these portfolios would I be comfortable owning based on its historical risk and return characteristics?"[46]

Asset Allocation — Risk & Reward
1926 - 2006

Average Return	Minimum Return	Largest Gain	Portfolio	Percentage Positive Years	Percentage Negative Years
-39%	10%	49%	90% Stocks / 0% Bonds / 10% Cash	72%	28%
-35%	10%	43%	80% Stocks / 10% Bonds / 10% Cash	73%	27%
-31%	9%	38%	70% Stocks / 20% Bonds / 10% Cash	77%	23%
-27%	9%	33%	60% Stocks / 30% Bonds / 10% Cash	77%	23%
-22%	8%	28%	50% Stocks / 40% Bonds / 10% Cash	78%	22%
-18%	8%	24%	40% Stocks / 50% Bonds / 10% Cash	80%	20%
-14%	7%	25%	30% Stocks / 60% Bonds / 10% Cash	86%	14%
-10%	6%	26%	20% Stocks / 70% Bonds / 10% Cash	90%	10%
-6%	6%	26%	10% Stocks / 80% Bonds / 10% Cash	94%	6%
-4%	5%	27%	0% Stocks / 90% Bonds / 10% Cash	90%	10%

Curian Capital, 2006

Let's assume you selected a portfolio of 50% stocks, 40% bonds, and 10% short-term investments. Now that we've decided on a portfolio whose historical risk and return characteristics we can comfortably live with, how do we determine how much we can safely withdraw each year?

A couple of qualifying notes are necessary here. Withdrawal planning is an inexact science. It is one of the great paradoxes of financial planning that past performance is no guarantee of future results, but the past is all we have to project future potential outcomes. There is no guarantee that your investment assets will grow at a certain rate or sustain any particular withdrawal percentage for a given period of time. There are many variables which must be considered such as age, life expectancy, asset allocation, taxes, and so on.

In order to help you think about withdrawal planning strategies, I have excerpted the following from the Trinity Study prepared by Philip L. Cooley, Carl M. Hubbard and Daniel T. Walz at Trinity University. Among other things, the study[47] analyzed inflation-adjusted withdrawal rates for various diversified portfolios from 1926–1995 to determine what withdrawal rate you could have historically sustained over a given time period. Let's look at it:

Likelihood of Sustaining a 30-year retirement
Inflation adjusted withdrawal rate as a % of initial portfolio value

● Bonds   ● Stocks

Withdrawal Rate	100% Bonds	25%/75%	50%/50%	25%/75%	100% Stocks
4%	83%	97%	96%	94%	92%
5%	30%	72%	82%	83%	82%
6%	3%	29%	57%	66%	69%
7%	0%	6%	30%	47%	54%
8%	0%	0%	13%	31%	41%

AAII Journal February 1998, Volume XX, No. 2, Philip L. Cooley, Carl M. Hubbard and Daniel T. Walz, Trinity University, San Antonio, Texas.

Let's take the portfolio of 50% stocks and 50% bonds as an example. If you selected a 5% annual withdrawal rate, you would have historically had an 82% chance of having your assets sustain you for thirty or more years. Now, this does not mean you should run out and place 100% of your retirement assets in stocks to ensure you receive the highest withdrawal rate. The devil, as they say, is in the details. What you should take away from the above chart is that both your asset allocation and your withdrawal rate are critical elements to ensure you don't outlive you assets by withdrawing too much too quickly. Withdrawal planning is more art than science. It requires constant attention, monitoring, and review. You will likely want to get some help in determining an appropriate asset allocation as well as an expected withdrawal rate for your personal circumstances.

Chapter Summary

♦   Developing an appropriate asset allocation and remaining flexible on your withdrawal rates are fundamental requirements for retirement planning.

♦   You simply must accept the fact that in order for your income to grow over time, your assets must grow as well.

♦   Designing asset allocations and withdrawal strategies is a complex process, and you should seriously consider getting some help with it.

21

H: Healthcare Strategy

The complexities of healthcare are vast and ever changing. In essence, healthcare expense in retirement represents an unknown liability. As I noted earlier, the projected out-of-pocket expenses for healthcare in retirement continue to increase, while health benefits from employers, Medicare, or private healthcare plans continue to decrease. This trend will not reverse itself in the foreseeable future and in all probability will get worse. As a result, it is imperative that you have a strategy to ensure unanticipated healthcare related expenses do not consume your retirement assets. In the interest of brevity, I will distill the requirements down to the most essential needs for a long and worry-free retirement. There are two general components of a healthcare strategy:

Primary healthcare

At the risk of oversimplifying, your primary healthcare needs revolve around three simple questions:

♦   What if I need to go to the doctor?

Your healthcare plan should provide for fixed costs to visit a primary care physician or specialist. These are typically referred to as "co-pays".

♦   What if the diagnosis requires me to purchase medication?

Your plan should include a prescription deductible that caps your costs for prescription medication, which is the overwhelming result of most initial visits to a physician.

♦   What if it's more serious and I have to go into the hospital?

Your plan should provide for a reasonable deductible that, once satisfied, has the insurance company assuming the responsibility for the rest of the hospital bills.

By ensuring that your healthcare plan has a fixed cost for physician visits, a prescription plan, and a hospitalization plan, you can minimize the likelihood that you have overlooked an essential element of primary healthcare coverage. If you are 65 or older and/or qualify for Medicare, then various elements of the Medicare plan currently provide for each of these conditions. Note that some of them come at an additional cost to you, so it's important to understand what is covered by basic Medicare versus supplemental Medicare plans available for additional purchase. It is advisable to seek professional assistance here to sort out the different coverage provided by the multitude of supplemental plans.

If you do not qualify for Medicare due to past employment, age, or other conditions, then you will need to rely upon private healthcare plans to meet these needs. These are typically provided through either prior employers or through private health insurance companies. Be sure your plan covers the three needs outlined above.

Long-term Care

If your diagnosis is more serious, you may require long-term care. Also known as nursing home care, this general term refers to your inability to perform what are referred to as "activities of daily living." These include eating, dressing, bathing, toileting, communicating, and other functions we take for granted each day. Note that I am not referring to "independent living" here. This term generally refers to those who still have the ability to manage for themselves when it comes to daily activities.

You should know that neither Medicare nor private healthcare plans provide for the costs of long-term care. Under current basic Medicare coverage, you are limited to 100 days of hospitalization. After this period, you will begin assuming the costs of care yourself. Sadly, surveys indicate that most people do not understand that having a spouse or other family member in long-term care means the family must foot the bill. The consequences to your retirement assets—or the assets of other family members—could be devastating.

If you decide to insure against long-term care needs, there are only two options from which you can choose: either purchase long-term care insurance or choose to "self-insure" by not purchasing it. Self-insurance simply means that you have ample savings earmarked for the expense should you, or a family member, require it. Either option can be fine, based on your personal circumstances. Depending upon where you live, long-term care expenses in a facility can range from $60,000 to $100,000 or more per year. Assuming an average stay of, say, three years, the cost could seriously compromise the retirement assets of most Americans. Assuming you choose to purchase insurance, long term-care insurance comes in two flavors—either pay-as-you-go premiums or a lump sum version referred to as asset-based long-term care. You will need to consult an advisor to determine which might be best for you.*

Long-term care is a healthcare liability not currently covered under any other primary health insurance plan. It's out there on its own as a risk, and you had better make a choice on how you plan to deal with it for the sake of your retirement assets and possibly your family's other assets. If you unconsciously choose to ignore it, you are consciously choosing to self-insure against it—whether you can afford it or not.

---

* Before you jump to the conclusion that I am somehow peddling long-term-care insurance, let me qualify my position on the matter: I care not whether you choose to self insure or purchase long-term care insurance—I only care that you make a conscious choice on a solution.

Chapter Summary

♦ **You absolutely must have a conscious healthcare strategy for the future. Your health and well being—and the financial health of your loved ones—may depend upon it.**

♦ **You must make a conscious choice regarding a Long-Term Care strategy. Simply ignoring it is financially irresponsible.**

22

E: Estate and Legacy Planning Strategy

There are three fundamental bases to cover here:

- Wills
- Trusts
- Insurance and risk management

In order to appease my publisher and various regulatory bodies, I am both compelled and delighted to profess that I do not offer legal or tax advice. Indeed, that's what attorneys and accountants are for. But, I can share with you the basic knowledge you need to consider for each of the above items to ensure you address them. Please note that it's not my purpose here to provide an exhaustive essay on the intricacies of wills and trusts. I'm simply trying to raise your awareness about the things for which you need to take personal responsibility. If this brief summary causes you to ask more questions of a qualified and competent professional, it's doing its intended job.

Wills

If you don't have one, shame on you. Get one. The cost of a basic will is nothing compared with the confusion, delay, and difficulty you can create for your beneficiaries by not having one.

First, let's define a few terms. When you die, all your stuff becomes your "estate". In many states, your estate goes directly to your spouse if you are married. But in many cases, your estate may need to be "probated." Probate is the legal process of settling the estate of a deceased person; specifically, resolving all claims and distributing your stuff. This is done by the probate court, which is responsible for making sure your stuff goes where it is supposed to based on your wishes and state laws.

Now, a fact hopefully not lost on you is that if you haven't left an official record of your wishes, the probate court has to figure it out without you. That can take time. A will simply instructs your heirs and the probate court how and to whom you wish to have your stuff distributed.[*] Now, why would you want to leave a legacy where strangers are tasked with figuring out who gets what?

Regarding expenses, probating your estate can involve probate court costs and legal fees. These vary by state, but it's not uncommon for them to total 3% to 6% of your estate value. Finally, note that your will becomes a matter of public record. This may or may not be of importance to you, but it's worth knowing. Once again, get a will. There's no excuse for not having one.

Trusts

Trusts come in many different forms, and their complexities are too broad to address here. But generally, a living trust may allow assets in the trust to pass to heirs without going through the probate process. In certain circumstances, this can save time and money. And, since it bypasses probate, it's private.

It is a common misconception that putting assets in a trust means you can no longer use them for your own benefit. This depends largely on the type of trust you create. Another common misperception is that by placing assets in a trust, you avoid onerous estate or (aptly named) death taxes. Once again, this is not necessarily the case. As of this writing, a number of laws regarding estate taxes are set to expire in the year 2010. Depending upon the size of your estate,

---

[*]   Simple enough?

these changes may or may not affect you. For people interested in a swift and private disposition of their estate, a trust can be a valuable vehicle.

In sum, you need to consult with a qualified estate planning attorney to determine what exactly is appropriate for your circumstances. Make sure the attorney specializes in estate planning, as the laws regarding estate planning change constantly.

Insurance and Risk Management

A word or two on insurance here is appropriate, because statistics show us that the majority of the population is significantly underinsured. Most people prefer not to think about insurance for a natural reason: The events that cause you to need it are generally unpleasant ones—disability, death, car accidents, a fire, illness, and so on.* We prefer not to think about such unpleasant things in the hope that they do not occur. We also hate paying for stuff we may never use.

For the moment, let's suspend any opinions we have of insurance in general. This means clearing your mind of images of seedy life insurance salespeople and big, greedy insurance companies. You need to understand three simple concepts—possibility, probability, and risk transfer.

Possibility means something may or may not happen. It is possible that you may die tomorrow, or next week. It is possible that your house may catch fire. Risks are inherent in life; we do not know when death, ill health, injury, or unemployment will occur. So, let's acknowledge that there are a whole series of possible events that could occur that would either disrupt or destroy your ability to provide for yourself or others in retirement. Agreed?†

Probability refers to the *chance* of something occurring. This is where the insurance company comes in. You acknowledge that there is a *chance* you could die in the next fifteen years, which would seriously disrupt and possibly destroy the opportunity for your spouse or heirs to live comfortably. A life insurance company—through much experience—knows roughly what the probability is that you may actually expire in this time period.‡

---

*   Right-brain stuff, to be sure.

†   If you take issue with this, I can recommend a good psychiatrist.

‡   Morbid, yes. But, stay with me.

Risk transfer refers to the ability for one party to transfer the risk of an event occurring to another party. Insurance companies allow you to transfer these risks to them in exchange for a payment or series of payments. The "possibility versus probability" principle is the basis for all insurance—life, disability, auto, homeowners, long-term care, etc. By purchasing insurance, you are not betting something *will* happen to you—you are acknowledging it is possible. Insurance companies agree to accept that risk—to let you transfer the risk to them. Let's talk for a moment about life insurance specifically. In my opinion, it has four potential uses for most people:

♦ Income replacement for a spouse or other dependents.

♦ Debt elimination for a spouse, dependents, or heirs.

♦ Creating a bigger estate for loved ones.

♦ Paying your estate taxes to Uncle Sam so your heirs get to keep what's in your estate.

Now, if you consider each of these and determine that your spouse or other dependents will have plenty of lifetime income from other sources, you have no significant debts to eliminate, you don't want to create a bigger estate, and you don't have an estate tax problem, then you might not have a need for life insurance.* It's quite simple to determine whether you need it or not. Imagine you die today. How would the financial lives of your family be affected? Would your pension go away and leave a spouse with limited income? Who would pay off the mortgage? Would your estate be subjected to a big tax bill, reducing its value to your heirs? If the answers are no, it's entirely possible you don't need it. If any of the answers are yes, you might need it.

For those of us who have been blessed with great financial success, life insurance can have many other creative uses for charitable planning, tax planning, and other more sophisticated strategies. Your personal circumstance will dictate whether any of those apply. An independent financial advisor can help you assess whether it's needed or not for any of the above. Regardless of your circumstances, it is incumbent upon you to absolutely ensure that all your insurance needs are covered, particularly if you plan to be around awhile.

---

* What, a financial advisor telling me not to buy something? The devil must be making snow cones, because hell hath surely frozen over.

Chapter Summary

♦ Leaving the disposition of your estate up to the courts is a horrible legacy to leave for your family members. If you don't have a will, get one. If you do have one, make sure it's current.

♦ The need for a trust is dependent upon your personal circumstances. You'll need some professional help to make a determination.

♦ Insurance of any kind is simply risk management. If you'd prefer to transfer the risk to someone else, buy insurance. If not, don't.

23

R: Review and Revise Annually

Change, as they say, is constant. When it comes to retirement planning there are three specific areas of change to monitor—the markets, the economy and your personal circumstances. It is important to review your RICHER™ Retirement Strategy annually to ensure all elements are current and accurate. Once your plan is in place, this annual review can be conducted with your advisor in about an hour. That's it. One hour every year. Most people spend more time planning their summer vacation. If, for some unfathomable reason you have elected to go it alone without an advisor, you'll need to pay a lot more attention to each area to ensure you've covered all the bases. After all, that's what you've engaged them to do for you.

Your annual review should encompass:

♦ **A review of your reserves to ensure you are maximizing your returns on your short-term assets.**

Are you getting the best rate available? Make sure you are reaping the maximum benefit on your dry powder. Remember, this is money we don't plan on using, but it's there in case we need it. Small differences in return can make a big difference over time. Be vigilant.

♦ **A review of your insured income cash flows and sources.**

Are there changes in your pension or Social Security income? What about your annuities? How much income do you anticipate needing in the next twelve months, and how much of it will come from your insured sources versus your capital growth and income strategy? You may find your need for insured income changes over time. Reviewing it annually gives you the opportunity to make adjustments as needed.

♦   **A review of your capital growth and income strategy.**

What was your investment experience for the past year? Does your asset allocation need adjustments based on market performance or personal circumstances? What is the outlook for the coming year? The markets are—by design—in a constant state of advance and decline. That's what makes them work for us. A well-designed portfolio should take this into consideration.

♦   **A review of your healthcare plans.**

Did you experience any changes to your primary healthcare plan, Medicare benefits, or other healthcare coverage? Are supplemental policies needed to fill in the gaps? Did any health-related issues develop that require adjustments to other parts of your strategy? Healthcare benefits change more rapidly—and will continue to do so. It's important to stay on top of your strategy and make adjustments accordingly.

♦   **A review of your estate planning elements.**

Are your wills and/or trust documents current? Have there been births, deaths, divorces in the family? Have you finally disowned that rotten nephew you felt sorry for a few years ago? These documents require an annual review to make sure your estate wishes are still intact.

Once you have your RICHER™ Retirement Strategy in place, it's easy to do a quick diagnostic check almost anytime. When you're sitting in traffic, relaxing by the pool, or weeding the garden, it's quite simple to run through the six key areas in your mind to make sure you're where you need to be.

Chapter Summary

♦ Things change. Your RICHER™ Retirement Strategy needs at least a comprehensive annual review to make sure it's up to date.

R: Reserve Strategy

I: Insured Income Strategy

C: Capital Growth and Income Strategy

H: Healthcare Strategy

E: Estate and Legacy Planning Strategy

R: Review and Revise Annually

Many receive advice, only the wise profit from it.

—Publilius Syrus

24

The Smartest Investment You Can Make

Whether you are anticipating your retirement or are already retired, the decisions you are making now with regard to your retirement assets will largely determine your destiny. The cost of sound counsel and advice can be much cheaper than the cost of unguided mistakes that compromise your future and the future of your family.

Permit me this one rant

I am constantly disappointed and frustrated by the myriad personal finance columnists and other self-appointed do-it-yourself experts who wish to convince you that every single financial advisor is nothing more than a wolf waiting to pounce upon you and turn your worthless portfolio into valuable trading commissions for themselves.

"Do it on your own," they cry from their newspapers, websites, and newsletters.

"Avoid anything you have to pay for," they shout, as they rake in subscription fees, advertising dollars, and proceeds from their book sales.

In my view, a columnist convincing an entire generation that retirement planning is easy to do on your own is tantamount to journalistic malpractice. First, remember that these folks haven't offered to help you personally. Generic musings on the pros and cons of annuities, mutual funds, stocks and bonds, or insurance have absolutely no application to your personal circumstances. Zero. Imagine a physician telling the entire world to take an aspirin for any ailment, regardless of a specific individual's condition or health history.

As for the do-it-yourself personal finance mavens, they certainly have no personal knowledge of or interest in your financial success. They, like their brethren in the newspapers and magazines, are selling something. In their case, it's books, online courses, cute DVD's, and handy financial organizers. (A word of caution: Preparing your own will or trust with a CD you ordered Sunday morning by calling an 800 number is a formula for trouble. It's not that easy, or estate-planning attorneys would be out of business.)

Finally, let's recall how these experts are compensated. They are paid based on book sales, advertising revenues, and speaking fees. None of them receive a greater or lesser reward if you're personally successful. They simply do not have a vested interest in your personal financial success. Don't believe me? Call one of them. "Well" you say, "I wouldn't expect them to take my call, because they are very busy." Right. So, you're going to take advice regarding your precious, hard earned assets from someone who is too busy to talk to you personally about it. Does that sound smart to you?

What these enlightened gurus of high finance fail to note is that most people don't want to do it themselves. They want help. And help doesn't come at the end of a phone line, on a website, or out of a box. It comes from an individual who knows you and understands your hopes, dreams, goals and objectives.

The funny thing about being a financial advisor is that the phone rarely rings when things are going well. It's when we experience the tough times that a good advisor earns his or her keep. Reminding our clients that we prepared their portfolio in anticipation of inevitable declines is where the rubber meets the road. Holding hands and reminding clients that advances and declines are to be expected, and that their investment strategy was prepared in anticipation of ebbs and flows, is where a good advisor is in their element. Ensuring that the next bear market does not compromise your retirement lifestyle is where a personal financial advisor shines. Reviewing and celebrating your progress with you as you accomplish milestones is where an advisor will bring you value.

Allow me to put the "you don't need any help to be financially successful" argument to bed with a simple question:

Where will your infomercial hawker, your 800 number advisor, and your financial columnist be when we experience (which we most certainly will) the next bear market? Will they be calling you to reassure you that their past advice, delivered en masse to thousands, still suits your personal needs? Will they hold your hand and explain that we expected this and that we prepared your financial plan accordingly?

Not likely.

There, I feel better. Thanks for listening.

Engaging a qualified financial professional to assist you can be the smartest investment you make. We have seen the track record of unguided investors as a group, and it's underwhelming. Of course, you are welcome to go it alone if you desire. Many people do. In our practice, we end up seeing many of them after it's too late to undo the damage they have caused to their portfolios, their lifestyle, and their legacy for future generations.

Now, how do you find a qualified advisor to help you?

If you have a failed relationship with a broker or financial advisor, I would venture to guess it's due to one of two reasons, or possibly both:

♦ You demanded something they couldn't deliver: *"I only want you to sell me tomorrow's top performing investments, and I'll give you my account."*

♦ He or she promised you something they could not deliver: *"My investment ideas will outperform any other broker or advisor you can find."*

Sound about right? The primary problem here is that these interactions are based on a transaction and a promise. It's a deal—not a relationship. What you need is an advisor who is interested in your success. One who wants to develop a relationship with you based on your long-term success and not on the next transaction. Here's a list of wrong things and right things in a relationship with an advisor. See where you feel most comfortable:

Your Advisory Relationship is driven by:

Buying and selling (Transactions)	Fees for services
Products	A Relationship
Promises of superior returns	Goals
Charts and Facts	Trust and Education

You need a leader, a coach, someone who can show you the future, and bring it back to the present while you can still do something about it. If your relationship with an advisor is based on the left side items, ultimately someone is going to end up disappointed. Focus on finding an advisor whose belief system is rooted on the right side items, and you'll stand a much better chance of getting where you're going on time with room to spare.

> *A qualified advisor can help you define your objectives, implement a retirement strategy, and monitor your progress and make changes as required.*

Hopefully, you understand by now that creating goals and objectives for retirement success is a process, not an event. So, you want a financial advisor who can serve as a guide for this important process. Another important reason for retaining a qualified advisor is this: The myriad of investments available to the average investor today is overwhelming. Further, many of these investment options can be quite detailed and complicated to understand. An advisor can help sort through the maze to ensure that, once your goals are defined, you hire the right investments to get you where you want to be.

The following is a list of attributes you will want to seek out in a financial advisor:

1. A Trusted Financial Advisor will always start out by defining your goals and understanding what you hope to accomplish. They represent a process, not a product. They will ask questions about your values and your goals as well as about your wallet.

2. A Trusted Financial Advisor is completely objective when selecting investments on your behalf. Using a limited list of investment options

created exclusively by an advisors firm is a warning sign.[*] Objectivity is a basic tenet of a financial advisors fiduciary responsibility to his or her clients. You will want to locate an advisor who has only one employer—you.

3. A Trusted Financial Advisor listens to you like you're the only person on the planet. Just like a physician, experienced advisors tend to talk less and listen more. In my view, the more an advisor insists on talking about their prowess and knowledge, the less they actually know about helping people.

4. A Trusted Financial Advisor will give you the plain, unvarnished truth—even when you might not want to hear it. The things you need to do to accomplish your retirement goals might not always be easy or comfortable, but every day you delay in starting will produce greater hardship down the road. You need honesty and candor.

5. A Trusted Financial Advisor will openly share with you how they are paid. As for you—price should only matter in the absence of value. What's it worth to you to get to your goals on time with room to spare? A great deal, I would hope. As we learned earlier, the cost you pay for good advice is much less than the expense you incur for mistakes.

6. A Trusted Financial Advisor has a code of ethics to which they strenuously adhere. Ask to see it. Any advisor worth their salt will have one.

7. A Trusted Financial Advisor believes in educating their clients. Constant contact, communication, and information sharing are necessary components of a long term mutually rewarding relationship.

Assuming this all makes complete sense to you, the questionnaire that follows this chapter will help you interview prospective financial advisors.

---

[*] The notion that one company could manufacture the best solutions for all your financial needs is nonsense.

Chapter Summary

♦ The cost of mistakes greatly exceeds the price of good advice.

♦ Finding a competent, qualified advisor just might be the smartest investment you can make.

Financial Advisor Interview Questionnaire

1) Please explain your philosophy on working with your clients.

2) What experience do you have?

3) Can you provide me with a copy of your SEC Form ADV?
    (a required regulatory document that explains an advisors services and fees.)

4) What industry credentials do you possess? How did you obtain them? (Be wary of mail order designations.)

5) Have you ever been disciplined for any reason in your professional career? Can I get it in writing?

6) Where will my assets be held?

7) Can you provide me with financial details on your organization?

8) Can I speak to a few of your other clients? Can I pick them randomly?

9) How are you paid for your services?

10) How often can I expect to meet with you?

Epilogue

When I set out to convey the messages in the book, I struggled with how exactly to do so without getting caught up in a bunch of dry statistical data. I'm pretty sure I failed at that, but I felt it was important to emphasize that the future will most certainly be challenging for many folks, and tried to provide hard evidence of this to make my case.

Hopefully, the irrefutable facts I shared in the first section of the book hit home in some way to readers. This is serious stuff, and you cannot wish it away or simply stick your head in the sand and ignore it. Throughout life, the actions—or inactions—of others impose themselves upon us in ways we may not see right away. Wars, terrorism, recessions, corporate malfeasance, governmental neglect, political incompetence—they affect every one of us in one way or another. Whether it's a personal loss, higher taxes, reduced benefits, or some other injustice, too often we simply attribute it to fate and move on.

The economic and demographic events and circumstances I highlighted are real. And, they are undoubtedly intersecting as we speak. What will the true outcome be? Will it be worse for you than I portrayed? I can't imagine it will be better without either divine intervention or you taking a higher level of personal responsibility for your outcome. That's where you come in.

You have the ability to change your future by simply acknowledging that you—and no one else—are responsible for your financial success and your security in retirement.

If you're ready to do so, I suggest you ensure you have a primary understanding of the basic, common sense guidelines presented herein for investment success. Then, find yourself a good advisor to guide you on your journey.

The measure of my success will be whether you are compelled to make some changes and take the responsibility seriously. If my efforts to motivate you to prepare yourself for a long, rich, and rewarding retirement have succeeded, then I will consider those efforts worthwhile.

I wish you nothing but the best in realizing your dream retirement.

End Notes

1. Mortality and Expense Tables, 2000; US Dept of Health and Human Services, "Health, United States", 2006.

2. Fidelity Investments Employer Services Study, 2007

3. National Coalition on Health Care, 2005

4. Department of Health and Human Services, January, 2005

5. DeNavas-Walt, Carmen, Bernadette D. Proctor, and Cheryl Hill Lee. "Income, Poverty, and Health Insurance Coverage in the United States: 2004." (Washington, DC: U.S. Department of Commerce, Economics and Statistics Administration, August 2005)

6. USA Today, "States Struggle to Cover Retirees", 12/18/06

7. IBID

8. Social Security Administration

9. 2004 Annual Report of the Board of Trustees of the Federal Old Age and Survivors Insurance and Disability Insurance Trust Funds

10. 2003 Annual Report of the Board of Trustees of the Federal Old Age and Survivors Insurance and Disability Insurance Trust Funds

11. The Policy Book: AARP Public Policies 2007

12. BBC News, November 30, 2006

13. "The Incredible Shrinking Benefits," *Business Week*, July 25, 2005

14. The New York Times, 11/6/2007, "Once Safe, Public Pensions Are Now Facing Cuts." Mary Williams Walsh.

15. Federal Reserve Board of Governors, National Personal Saving Rate and Household Financial Wealth; 3/02

16. USA Today, "Rate of Savings Among Americans Continues to Fall", October 6, 2006

17. Center for Retirement Research, Boston University, "Will We Have to Work Forever?" July, 2006

18. Retirement Research Center, University of Michigan, "Baby Boomer Retirement Security: the Roles of Planning, Financial Literacy, and Housing Wealth" 2006, *Gustman and Steinmeier 2004; Bernheim 1998*

19. Profitable Prudence: The Case for Public Employer Defined Benefit Plans, Gary W. Anderson and Keith Brainard. Pension Research Council. The Wharton School of the University of Pennsylvania.

20. Dr. Richard Johnson, Retirement Options, 2005

21. Metlife Study of Employee Benefit Trends, 2005

22. Gallup Organization, 2005

23. Saving Matters, US Dept of Labor, Sept., 2006

24. Remember When: 1950, A Nostalgic Look Back in Time, Seek Publishing

25. * CDA Wiesenberger, 1/06. ** Highest marginal Federal income tax rate based on $100,000 of taxable income for a married couple filing jointly. www.taxpolicycenter.org.

26. Hartford Life Insurance Company, 2005

27. Example assumes a 7% average annualized rate of return on a $250,000 value. The columns demonstrate the impact of the sequence of returns assuming 5% annual withdrawals of $12,500 increasing 3% annually for inflation. Past performance does not guarantee future results. Source: Prudential, 2006.

28. Congressional Budget Office, 2001

29. Bureau of Labor Statistics, Department of Commerce, 2/02. Segal Health Plan cost Survey, 2002.

30. Federal Office of Personnel Management, Inquiry Journal, Winter, 2005

31. Marketwatch, Retirement Weekly, September 29, 2006

32. Dalbar. Quantitative Analysis of Investor Behavior update, 2004

33. "Dumb Money: Mutual Fund Flows and the Cross-Section of Stock Returns", Andrea Frazzini and Owen Lamont, 2005.

34. Susan Pluch and Jeff Kelly, Going Against the Crowd, Morningstar Mutual Funds, Jan. 1996, Vol 4, Number 5

35. CPI Inflation Calculator, NASA.gov

36. "Popularity Contests for Contrarians", Carole Gould, New York Times, March 9, 1997

37. On January 3, 1995, the S&P 500 stood at 470. At the close of 2003, it was 1,111, producing an average annual return of 11.3%. Source: Yahoo! Finance.

38. Brad Barber and Terrance Odean, "The Common Stock Performance of Individual Investors," Journal of Finance, April, 2000

39. Klaus Kiss and Jenny Jordan, Advertising in the mutual fund business: The role of judgmental heuristics in private investors evaluation of risk and return", Journal of Financial Services Marketing. Nov 2002.

40. USA Today, November 1, 2006

41. Kinder Institute of Life Planning, "A Life Planning Methodology for the Coming Revolution in Client Relationships", Journal of Financial Planning, April, 2005

42. Bryan Olson; Center for Investment Research, Charles Schwab & Co.,2005

43. Franklin Templeton Investments,2006

44. Rolling time periods for the S & P from 1926–2003, CD Wiesenberger, 1/04

45. Credit ratings are provided by independent ratings agencies such as A.M. Best, Standard and Poors, Moody's and others.

46. The chart data was derived from back tested performance of hypothetical portfolios. Portfolio returns represent the weighted average annual return for each asset class. Stock performance is represented by the historical performance of the S&P 500 Index. Bond performance is represented by the historical total return of intermediate term US Government Bonds. Cash equivalents are represented by the historical total return of 30-day US Treasury Bills. Source: Curian Capital.

47. AAII Journal February 1998, Volume XX, No. 2, Philip L. Cooley, Carl M. Hubbard and Daniel T. Walz, Trinity University, San Antonio, Texas.